Our Covenant

The 2000–01 Minns Lectures

The Lay and Liberal Doctrine of the Church:
The Spirit and the Promise of Our Covenant

ISBN: 0-9702479-2-3

Editing, design, and layout by Laura Horton

Our Covenant

The 2000–01 Minns Lectures

The Lay and Liberal Doctrine of the Church:
The Spirit and the Promise of Our Covenant

by

Alice Blair Wesley

Table of Contents

Foreword 1

Lecture 1 5
Love Is the Doctrine of This Church
*Delivered on November 12, 2000 at First Church and Parish,
Dedham, MA*

Lecture 2 25
Thus Do We Covenant
Delivered on November 15, 2000 at First Parish, Brookline, MA

Lecture 3 45
How We Came to Forget the Covenant for a Long Time
*Delivered on February 22, 2001 at the Institute for Ecumenical
Theological Studies, Seattle University, Seattle, WA*

Lecture 4 65
The Theology and Anthropology of Our Liberal Covenant
*Delivered on February 25, 2001 at University Unitarian Church,
Seattle, WA*

Lecture 5..83
Updating the Cambridge Platform
Delivered on April 6, 2001 at All Souls Unitarian Church,
Tulsa, OK

Lecture 6...101
Toward a Covenanted Association of Congregations:
On Patterns of Authentic Authority among Free Churches
Delivered on April 7, 2001 at All Souls Unitarian Church,
Tulsa, OK

Reading List..121

Foreword

Right at the start I may as well just blurt out two facts, which must stand awkwardly together in reference to a third. (1) For a very long time now we liberals have bad-mouthed—even demonized—our spiritual ancestors, the Puritans who founded our oldest Unitarian Universalist churches in New England. (2) I have come to love these 17th-century ancestors of ours, to respect them greatly, and to feel profoundly indebted to them for the precious heritage of congregational polity, the theological and religious roots of which we have too long ignored. (3) I hope to persuade you that we UUs urgently need to reclaim and freshly adapt for our time the radically covenantal doctrine of the free church with which our UU history on the North American continent began in the 1600s.

That last is the challenge I've taken up. I'm out to contest old prejudices against our past, to provoke a critical and constructive review of some of our present practices, and to call for a forward-looking re-formation that Unitarian Universalist congregations might fulfill our great promise. Printed here are the six Minns Lectures I delivered in the church year 2000–01, on the theme of the covenant of the free church and its past and present history, theology and governance. Scattered throughout, you will find various pieces of an explanation of why I took up such a sprawling, multi-faceted topic. I hope it will suffice here to say I believe we human beings can't appreciate, understand deeply or defend what we take for granted. We have long so taken congregational polity for granted that we haven't even tried for a long time to think carefully together about our organization. We have not so much chosen as drifted into contradictory and inappropriate institutional practices. These practices have made us,

1

and are keeping us, weak and small. Finally, I propose some changes I believe can lead to stronger liberal churches, richly meaningful to many more people.

The Minns Lectureship was endowed in the 1940s by a member of First and Second Church in Boston. Members of the Minns Committee come from both First and Second Church and King's Chapel. Each year the Committee chooses one "Unitarian minister in good standing" to deliver six lectures. Over the decades many of our finest ministers have given the Minns Lectures.

I am humbly grateful to every one of the following people: The Rev. Richard Henry and my husband Joe Wesley overcame my reluctance and insisted that I submit a proposal to the Minns Committee. Members of the Minns Committee, chaired at the time by the Rev. Diane Arkawa, invited me to add my name to a distinguished list of predecessors. The ministers and members of the four of our churches and the administrative staff of a university where the 2000–01 Minns Lectures were given all extended wonderfully cordial hospitality—at the First Church and Parish in Dedham and First Parish in Brookline, MA; Seattle University and the University Unitarian Church in Seattle, WA; and All Souls Unitarian Church in Tulsa, OK. The Rev. Ken Oliff urged and saw through the Lectures' publication on Meadville/Lombard's online *Journal of Liberal Religion*. The Rev. Dr. Bill Murry, president of Meadville/Lombard Theological School, and his fine staff have seen this text into print under the aegis of the Meadville/Lombard Press.

There were certainly some scholars in my audiences, but my intention was to address our laity, people of enormous intelligence and dedication, but whose life work is not church history or liberal doctrine. So I dispensed altogether with the scholarly apparatus of footnotes. Some citations are noted in the text. A reading list is appended.

I have wanted the printed text to retain as much as possible the flavor of oral delivery. The italics in the print indicate some of the oral stress I added when I read the text aloud to live audiences. Those who heard the lectures in person and the nearly 500 people who asked for and have received copies via e-mail will find few changes beyond the correction of typos and some very occasional shortening by a few words here and there.

If you like to know something of an author before you read, here are a few pertinent facts about this one. I am a graduate of the University of Louisville. I began studies for our ministry at age 36. At that time I had long been an active lay UU and a schoolteacher. I was also mother of two and wife of a rising, often-transferred young engineering manager. From 1973 to 1977 I was a special (non-credit) student at Meadville/Lombard, and I also took courses yielding 30 graduate credits at Lamar University in Beaumont, TX. For twenty years I served congregations in Texas, Maryland and New Jersey, most often as an extension or new congregation minister. The fact of my life that I am proudest of—apart from my family—is that all eight of the congregations I served are still today larger and stronger than they were when I joined them, in no small measure because of the ministry that members and I were able to do together.

Over the years I served on or chaired numerous District, Summer Institute and UUMA committees and boards. I many times addressed and/or led workshops at summer institutes and the Mountain's leadership training school. I was for four years president of UU Advance and founded *First Days Record*, a journal for UU ministers. Published articles of mine have appeared in *First Days Record*, the *Register/Leader*, the *World*, the *Journal of the Liberal Ministry*, *Kairos*, the *UU Christian* and *UUMA Essays*. I published two editions of one other book, in 1987 and 1988, *Myths of Time and History: A Unitarian Universalist Theology*, which was used in quite a few church study groups. I retired in 1996. Currently, my husband and I live in both Allentown, PA and Bellevue, WA to be near our four fine grandsons. In both places I help to edit the online *Dictionary of UU Biography*, a project of the UU Historical Society, headed up by the Rev. Peter Hughes.

I don't expect at all that you will agree with everything you read here, or that the changes I urge will be all or soon adopted. I do hope the understanding and vision of the free church described here might serve as a yeasty leavening of the lively, potent liberal churches ours yet may be.

Allentown, PA
March 14, 2002

Lecture 1:
Love Is the Doctrine of This Church

Love is the doctrine of this church,
The quest of truth is its sacrament,
And service is its prayer.
To dwell together in peace,
To seek knowledge in freedom,
To serve human need,
To the end that all souls shall grow into harmony with
    the Divine—
Thus do we covenant with each other and with God.

You recognize one of the most frequently used readings in our hymnal. This short text, or a variation of it, is and has long been a part of every Sunday service in many of our strongest churches. The covenant of the free church, given expression in these words, is the key to an understanding of our churches' continuity over the centuries, since the 1630s when our oldest churches were founded here. I'll say that another way. We North American Unitarian Universalists, in all our diversity, share one doctrine everywhere in common, with each other now and with our earliest church ancestors on this continent. We call it the doctrine of congregational polity. We would better call it the doctrine of covenantal organization. For the design of free churches' organization is simply a logical consequence of the theological character of their members' covenant. It's very important to keep polity and covenant clearly connected. At present very few UUs know how the doctrine of congregational polity ever came to be ours. Moreover, the disconnect among us between polity and covenant is one of long standing. Our organizational ineptness over the centuries, up to the present, is best understood as a product of this disconnect. My aim in these lectures is to trace the history of the covenant and the organization of our free churches on this continent and to reconnect them in our understanding.

In this first lecture I'll tell you how I came to see our organizational strengths and weakness as I do, and then address the question: Where does that first line, "Love is the doctrine of this church," come from, historically?

I sought your invitation to give the first of the 2000–01 Minns Lectures in the First Church, Dedham, Massachusetts. I hope you will see, as we go along, why I so much wanted to begin here. It is because a very quiet little event—of long, still living, tradition-shaping consequence—happened here among a small group of ancestors of today's Unitarian Universalists, in 1637.

This quiet little event was meant to lead to the founding of the Dedham Church. It did. Moreover, it led to the founding in 1638 of a particular *kind* of free church, having distinct features, very characteristic of other free churches already founded and soon to be founded all over the region by the 20,000 or so colonists who came to New England by the shipload in the decade of the 1630s, specifically for the purpose of founding just this kind of free church.

I don't myself know how many church communities these 20,000 New Englanders organized, in what they called "the liberty of the Gospel." But 200 years later, during a period of about 50 years—from roughly 1820 to 1870—some 125 of these churches, one by one, took the name Unitarian, including First Church, Dedham, one of the earliest to do so. These New England ancestors of ours set the institutional patterns in which, still today, all our Unitarian Universalist congregations are individually organized. Our institutional history begins in the 1630s.

Now everything that happened here in New England in the 1630s was but one fruit of a great sprawling complex of earlier and continuing events elsewhere, in Europe in the 1500s and 1600s. Those events involved much noise, a lot of very confused politics, and everywhere varying amounts of violence, even unto international war. I mean that vast complex of events known as the Protestant Reformation. But I want to focus on the long meanings of this one small, tradition-shaping event, way over on the left wing of the Reformation, as those meanings have a bearing now, on the liberal Unitarian Universalist congregations of North America.

For I say—whether you ever heard, directly, of this little event in Dedham or not—to understand in any depth our liberal free church tradition, or to make much sense of deeply rooted everyday realities of Unitarian Universalist churches now, today, you must understand in your bones the historical importance of the *spirit of love* manifest in the doctrine of covenantal organization, as this little group of people in Dedham understood it in New England, in 1637.

But I should make here a confession. I shall "hold forth" as a lay theologian, not a scholar. Scholars are life-long students of some many-faceted subject, whose habits of mind are neat. Scholars have practiced for years the minute tasks of making good notes and carefully filing them for later access. A scholar's mind has slowly come to resemble a well-catalogued library. I have spent many years studying our liberal religious tradition and churches—as a lay member, a seminarian and a parish minister. My mind, though, does not much resemble a library. My mind is more like an old family attic.

I have often ruefully wished I were a scholar. But I have spent my forty-odd years as a Unitarian Universalist mostly in active—some might say hyperactive—engagement with other church members, in 16 of our congregations, in Kentucky, Delaware, Texas, Maryland, New Jersey and, of late, Washington State and Pennsylvania. I have been briefly in and out of the buildings and lives of many more of our churches, from Georgia to British Columbia and from Maine to California.

Of course, I have also spent, in my forty years as a UU, a good deal of time closeted with books, off by myself, reading, pondering, trying to get some handles on the meaning of our churches' very mixed bag of strengths and weakness, fine success and sad failure to thrive more vigorously. In my hunt for some handles, I have been, then, mentally much in and out of our churches in New England, trying to understand the paths our people have traveled that led to where we are now.

7

But the truth is, I never stayed closeted long enough to do much filing. Instead, I always rushed off to another meeting, or counseling session, or worship service—to engagement with other members. So, my studies of our history have always had more of a rummaging than a scholarly quality. You know how it is on a hunt for something up in the attic. It's a kind of round-and-roundabout-again exercise in frustration and delight. You start, thinking you'll go through these dusty old boxes to find one thing. First thing you know, though you haven't found that one thing, you've got a hodgepodge of really interesting, happily chanced-upon old family things lying about, pulled from various boxes, and the doorbell rings. Later, the next time you can get back up there, you go through the same process, only now arranging little stacks of stuff there and about, while still looking for that one thing, and a telephone call ends that day's research. Such have mostly been my times of study. That is partly what I mean by saying I am a lay theologian.

But there's more to it. When I say I am a lay theologian, I mean that for longer now than 25 years, my rummaging in our history has always centered—more or less—on a hunt for the *lay doctrine* of our free and liberal churches. What ought all the *lay* members of a liberal free church understand their own local congregation to be about? Answer that, and you can discuss the liberal doctrine of the church. That is, you can have a lucid conversation about the doctrine our members should *teach* concerning their own thriving, livewire liberal church, by what they say and by their actions in the church. For that is what a doctrine is: A doctrine is a *lived teaching* about the essential nature of something. So, this is my question: *What ought the lay members of a liberal free church understand our kind of church to be about, now, in our time?* And however far afield in time I may get in parts of this discussion, I mean this to be the one issue of these lectures. Here's how this question became central for me.

For one academic winter term I was lucky enough, at age 36, to be part of a seminary class taught by James Luther Adams at Meadville/Lombard Theological School in Chicago. The course was titled "Liberal Doctrine of the Church." Jim Adams traced in his lectures and class discussions dozens and more dozens of factors involved in the historical development of our liberal churches. Yet, his classes always had one paramount theme, which I summarize: Strong, effective, lively liberal churches, sometimes capable of altering positively the direction of their whole society, will be those liberal churches whose lay members can say clearly, individually and collectively, what are their own most important loyalties, as church members.

Note: *Not* what are their beliefs, as in a creedal church. Rather, what are their shared, mutual *loyalties* in a *covenantal* church.

I don't know any of Adams's students who can describe briefly what he could do to your head. The only world-class theologian North American Unitarian Universalists produced in the 20th century, Adams had the ability to lay his hand on the time horizon of a student's mind and give it a swift yank. The sudden expansion of *relevant* time was breath-taking. For JLA—as his students called him—was not interested only in the modern, the current version of the liberal free church. He wanted us to learn how there ever came to be such a thing as a free church and, moreover, what was going on during those crucial events of history, when a few people—loyally holding onto the idea of the free church, in face of nearly overwhelming opposition—when a few people in little religious groups made fateful decisions, which reshaped the tradition not only of the free church, but, eventually, of all Western culture.

Why did JLA so much want us to learn about the roots of our liberal church tradition? Because this is simply a fact: *The modern liberal free church grew, very slowly, out of earlier free churches.* And, as novelist William Faulkner said, "The past is not dead. It's not even past."

The still living consequences of our spiritual ancestors' convictions—both their convictions that were "right on" and are still in accord with reality, and their mistaken convictions, based then and still based on inadequate readings of the human situation—the consequences of our ancestors' convictions live on in us most often as *unexamined assumptions,* some of them inadequate, mistaken, not life-enhancing, even deadening. So, while we have inherited, though we may hardly realize it, some wonderful consequences of their "right on" convictions, we have also inherited warping consequences of our ancestors' mistakes which show up in *our* weak, or warped, or nearly dysfunctional, maybe dying churches. All that is part of our tradition, which has made and makes us now, who we are as liberal churchpeople.

Often you may hear UUs speak of ours as "the free church," as though ours are the only such. We may speak of in a fashion implying that our tradition has nothing to do with any older—we mean those "outmoded"—traditions of other churches. It was a major mission of James Luther Adams to make his students understand that the naive and arrogant assumptions, underlying any such talk, are arrant nonsense, warping nonsense. The more we believe it, the more it weakens us.

Many a liberal student—including yours truly—entered one of JLA's courses assuming that liberal churches sprang up, sort of like mushrooms, overnight—maybe in the 1820s, maybe in the 1930s, or even later. Anyway very recently, as history goes. Anything that happened before that time is "ancient history" having practically nothing to do with the modern liberal church. Supposing ourselves "broad-minded," we were in fact—as JLA would say—"temporally parochial." The very word liberal means free to think broadly, but we were, in our thinking about liberal religion, not really broad-minded, but narrow-minded, limited to the confines of a narrow little slit of time, recent decades, actually.

And suddenly, there you were in a JLA class, listening as he showed you, illumined for you—with his endless stories—the many direct links between other long ago and faraway crucial times and events of today. For the modern liberal church is but one of many groups belonging to the great tradition of the free church. The great tradition of the free church reaches—not reached—reaches, still lives, in a stretch of at least 4000 years of human history, not a mere 70 or 180 years. So, JLA's lectures ranged over the continents and back and forth in time, lighting here on yesterday's newspaper headlines, there on the writings of an Old Testament prophet, touching briefly on the craft guilds of medieval Europe, back to the hierarchical governments of ancient Mideast empires, and on to what happened in 1947 at a board meeting of a local Unitarian church. Or, as JLA used to say, "There is no such thing as the immaculate conception of an idea."

With reference to the liberal doctrine of the church, JLA meant that whenever the lay members of a liberal, lively and effective local church can speak clearly of their own shared loyalties, neither their achievement of such clarity nor the splendid power of their congregation richly to enhance human lives is rightly understood if you think of it as something easily or only recently available to modern liberals. Certain visitors—potential members—may find what the members say is so patently clear that the whole idea of an authentically liberal free church may seem like just very appealing common sense. And these will join and become active members.

But in truth, the simple, transparent, potent idea of the free church has had to be, time and time and time again, re-conceived, re-constructed in human imagination, from memories of the tradition so obscured, or twisted and bent out of shape over time, as to be—sometimes—almost gone from the world. Moreover, the free church has never been reconceived and re-formed other than in the midst of some very particular era, when the reformers were caught up—as all human beings always are—in confused and confusing, complex and complicated events of their own particular times, in the messiness of human social intercourse. All ideas are born of human social intercourse. There is no such thing as the "immaculate conception" of any idea, including the idea of the free church.

So really, no matter how neat may be their study habits, even great scholars never can find in the records any perfect sample of the free church, one item we have only to lift from a box neatly labeled, "Documents of the Free Church." For the free church never has been and is not now perfectly manifest in any religious group—and not in ours either. That is the very nature of an ideal.

We cannot ever fully realize or institutionalize the ideal free church. Why? Well, for many reasons. The most important one, by far, is this: Our human loyalties are hardly ever quite as clear to ourselves as we may think they are. *Only the consequences of widely characteristic events of any one era can to some extent disclose the actual human loyalties shaping events of a particular time.* Jesus is said to have said, "By their fruits ye shall know them." Well, sure. But very often the fruits of what we do today don't show up for a long time. And besides the problem of delayed results, when the "fruits" of human choices and actions are "born," they come to fruition all mixed in

11

with a lot of other stuff. Which can make it really hard to tell what the heck we are doing, right now, every Sunday and every day.

Take just one example of what can happen in a liberal free church. The picture, of recent events I shall describe in one church, is sufficiently like—I dare say—the picture of similar events in many Unitarian Universalist churches, that thousands of UUs would recognize this picture and say—"Yep, I know that church. As hard as the devil to change, too. Try to change it and you may get 'killed'!"

Just 12 or 15 years ago, in the late 1980s, there was a small UU congregation of about 70 members. Call it the Little Valley Church. If you asked the members to describe their liberal church, they would tell you, sincerely and with one voice, "Our church stands for individual freedom of thought." If you then asked, "Is that what makes yours a good church?" the members would answer, again with one voice, "A church is really just people. Our members are wonderful, interesting, caring people. That's why ours is a good church."

Well, the Little Valley Church was then, in the late '80s, about 30 years old and sitting right in the middle of an area which had become, in the last 15 years, a far-out suburb of a large city, with a rapidly growing and increasingly liberal population—*i.e.*, their county had changed a lot in the last 15 years. Back when the church was still new, 30 years earlier, their mostly rural and conservative county had three small towns. The church back then, drawing members from all over the county, had flourished remarkably. They had a lively church school on Sundays and a much larger art school for children during the week. Members started an art fair, which soon grew to be so huge the County Parks Department had to take it over. And, most remarkably, in this conservative area members of that church were largely responsible, in the late '60s and '70s, for ending racial segregation in the county schools and restaurants. Several members were long-time friends of the county's African American leaders. A few church members were African American. Sound great? It *was* a great little liberal church!

By the late '80s the county had been booming steadily for 15 years, but the little liberal church never grew. By then, about 40% of the members were 70 years old or more. The church school was tiny. There was almost no church activity during the week. The grass outside might get to be a foot tall before it was mowed. What in the world happened?

Well, with all the good stuff they did, here's what else went on. Members of the Little Valley Church for 30 years loyally persevered, not in life-enhancing acts of devotion to freedom of thought in their church, but in stupefyingly dull acts of waiting out the "talkback." The talkback, together with announcements, took up at least half the service every Sunday. Think of it! Multiply thirty minutes by 40 Sundays a church year by 30 years! That's a lot of dull and boring time. But every Sunday, all the members present patiently waited for two, just two long-winded, very sarcastic individuals—who disagreed about everything under the sun—at long last to run down and hush. For not until they did, could the leader of the day say the "closing words," after which all could at last move on to "coffee hour."

I must tell you they did much good ministry in coffee hour, which might well last an hour, and also during monthly potluck luncheons which could last up to 3 hours. These were loving people; they enjoyed each other and helped each other out a lot. But freedom of thought in the liberal church, they thought, implied a strict rule to be rigidly observed, a kind of Law: Members of a liberal church *must* listen to hours and hours and hours of sheer blather. And they all did, not to anyone's benefit, but in loyal accord, they thought, with the tradition of the liberal free church.

What sort of loyalty was actually at work here? Neither of the two persons who dominated Sunday services cared two hoots, really, about freedom of thought in the liberal church. These two just loved to argue, about anything, in front of an audience. They really never noticed how seldom other members of the congregation—the free church gathered for worship—took part in these unending harangues. They never changed each other's or anybody else's thought. No issue was ever resolved and followed by some earnest action. Indeed, there was precious little exercise of freedom of thought, during their worship services, having any non-trivial purpose. And the members of the Little Valley Church wondered why their church—which had lots of visitors—never grew!

Moreover, the members' addiction to informality brought with it an even more serious problem, one entirely invisible. I mean the problem of

13

authority in the free church: *Who gets to decide what in the free church? When? Why?* At those long coffee hours and potluck luncheons, the whole atmosphere looked friendly and relaxed, as if these people had no leadership. They did. They had a highly authoritarian, secret ringleader, who by the late '80s had been exercising illegitimate power in the church for at least their most recent 15 years, maybe throughout their 30 years as a church, although nobody knew it. This is what was happening.

With the growing population of the county came a few UUs from more active churches elsewhere. These few newer members often brought up, during coffee hour, ideas of things it would be good to do in the church. Others might respond with some enthusiasm. Then what? Nothing. So, the few newer members were always saying to one another, "The people here are awfully nice. I really like them, but they won't *do* anything. Why?"

The fact is they *couldn't* do anything. Because, given the rigid informality of their church organization, it was easy as pie for one ringleader of a little group of three or four old friends—charming people, everybody loved them—to get together, maybe just on the phone, during the week. These few would decide privately, "No, we don't want to do such-and-such; it would cost too much." Or, "We tried that years ago, remember; it didn't work out." Or, "Not many people in our church are really interested that sort of thing."

Then each of these three or four called two or three other members, their special friends. Thus, all new ideas were quashed, routinely, systematically, thoroughly. Whoever raised an idea never knew why, at the next coffee hour, it was just not to be discussed. Bring it up again, and the conversation just moved pleasantly on to other matters, as inexorably as late afternoon moves toward night.

Empowerment, of both individuals and groups, happens within certain patterns of organization. Unless these patterns are both visible and widely familiar, nobody knows who can properly do what, and so nobody feels empowered. Whenever there is too much informality in free church organization, trouble—bad trouble—is at hand. For in an informal organization, authority is not clearly delegated, with members exercising their freedom of thought to decide who might best head up or coordinate this or that task, or why it might be good for several subgroups to take up different tasks, or why we might need to alter how all our subgroups connect, and thus work both separately and together.

In fact, in a very informal little church there *aren't* any fructifying and complementary sub-groups. So the members become, not an organized body, walking toward some chosen goals—with arms carrying, legs walking, lungs taking in air, eyes reading the road signs and so on. The members become just an amorphous collection of individuals sort of milling about, as in coffee hour. In the Little Valley Church, this had come to pass because one undelegated ringleader had an invisible hammerlock on all the decision-making authority in that church. Even officers were really elected only *pro forma*. And this ringleader loved—what? Freedom of thought? She loved her authority and power—in a corrupted liberal free church—as much as any Roman Catholic pope ever loved his. *The informal church organization only looks free; it is actually rigidly hierarchical and authoritarian.*

A case in point, then. The lay members of that church could not say clearly what were their own mutually shared loyalties. Actually, they were primarily loyal as churchpeople to two things: 1) loosely expressed, often meanly expressed, meaningless opinions and 2) informality. So, the church was stuck, irrelevant to their county, not doing anything much but taking care of each other, caught in the shallows of unconscious hypocrisy, and slowly dying.

Friends, we Unitarian Universalists deceive ourselves if we falsely suppose that only older churches, established in the 4th or the 16th or the 18th centuries—not modern liberal churches established in the 19th or 20th or 21st centuries—can deserve to be called "outmoded," drugged by the thin fumes of a not profound liberalism—and dying. A devoted friend of our churches, a UUA Officer, used to say to me in the late '80s, "We've got hundreds of churches already dead. They just haven't fallen over yet." Sadly, she was right. We UUs are beneficiaries and bearers of the great tradition of the free church. It is, at once, an exceedingly strong and precious and a fragile inheritance. We stand in just as much danger of losing it as any other church ever has or ever will—in a haze of confusion and forgetfulness.

15

But hey, I'm not about to deliver a jeremiad here, to make you feel really down about the state of some of our churches. Here's a P.S. to the story of the Little Valley Church. In the late '80s things began to change there. Then it began to grow, significantly. More changes followed growth. And with these changes came a full measure of baffling "dust and heat," as hard for members to understand as anything that had ever happened among them. The truly beloved ringleader left, very angrily, and took about 16 other loved members with her. It was a painful and wrenching big loss for so small a group. But the church kept on growing, bought a new site and put up a fine new building to make possible more growth still. Since their dying time of 12 or 15 years ago, the membership has nearly tripled. Their members now can say much more clearly than they used to, what are their commonly shared loyalties. Freedom of thought in the church now means much more than it once did. That's why it is still growing.

The doctrine—the lived teaching—of a free church entails several crucial elements. One of the most important has to do with *patterns of delegated authority*, both in local churches and among churches belonging to our Association. In times of weakness we always need to look to see if there aren't some very poor patterns of authority among us, of long standing. Remember: I am always talking about patterns of authority affecting the *lay* members of the local church, the people who, from the time they join, intend to—and do—attend services together, plan and work together and socialize together—often and continuously over the years of their lives. I will later try to show something of how and why healthy and open delegation of authority became the difficult problem it has long been for us, throughout much of our movement's history. I hope I have so far illustrated this: *Most crucially, the doctrine of a free church flows from mutually shared loyalties of the members, and these loyalties are to be seen at work in everything the members do together as churchpeople.*

But what loyalties, specifically? So far, I've only talked about loyalty to meaningful freedom of thought in the church. Is that it? No. That formulation of the issue doesn't cut to the heart of any specifically *religious* issue.

I just told of some good—not bad, good—people who came pretty close to killing off their own church because they loved most, in the church, the wrong things. They forgot that freedom in the church is not of much use or value *unless freedom is there used to explore, together, the realities of our lives we find most worthy of faithful love*. For all their easy talk of freedom, these members had not consciously, for a generation, linked freedom in the church with religious love of the most worthy realities of their lives, the kind of love so deep that it informs and shapes all our loyalties, inside and outside the church.

Here's a little question some in the world might consider innocent. Why not have the programs of a liberal church efficiently run and managed by a hired agent of our democratic government, *e.g.*, the Department of Health and Human Services? Or, an agent from one of the big non-profit corporations? The Red Cross, the YMCA or the YMHA? We'd surely have as many pleasant coffee hours and potluck dinners and more good lectures and discussions.

Why do we here in this Unitarian church inwardly scream "No!" at the mere suggestion of having our churches run by *any* outside corporate bureaucracy, no matter how benign—even one of our own devising, the UUA? The reason is this. No matter how much we Unitarian Universalists may have changed since New England colonists established the free church tradition in our part of the world in the 1630s, we have not changed in this: We understand way down deep that freedom in the church—and the authority to run it and do in it what we, the local members, deem best—is absolutely necessary and must be inviolable if we are to have in our lives one community, among all those of which we are a part, in which we can—with honest, though sometimes conflicted hearts and minds—examine together our own deepest loves. We need to examine together our own deepest loves, that we can try to see whether we are living by *right* loves, or by some misplaced, inappropriate love for less than worthy realities.

Another popular reading in our hymnal is titled, "It Matters What We Believe." That statement is true, but it matters most what we love. The free church is an organization we establish and join so that we may help each other to find, over and over again, in a thousand varying time frames and settings, what are our own worthiest loves, and therefore, what these loves now require of us, if we would be loyal in the most meaningful

17

sense, in what we do, in our actions, in the way we live. The basic enterprise of the free church is too personally important ever to turn over to any but faithful, long-term partners in the business of living with religious integrity—the living out of our real and right loves.

Now I want to tell you what happened here in Dedham, in 1637, before the founding of the Dedham Church, the same church in whose building we are meeting in the year 2000. The story is recorded in the *First Church Records*, Book I, now kept in the archives of the Dedham Historical Society.

By 1637 there were about 30 families in Dedham, all very recently settled here. They had come from various parts of England. Some families had even lived for a while—since they got off different ships—in various of the new towns, until the General Court said that the people in these 30 or so families could have a parcel of land, a township to be named Dedham.

Upon reaching this piece of the American wilderness, they first had to design a town government, so they could decide how legally to allot fields for growing crops and smaller lots for the building of houses. Then, with pens built for their animals, initial crops seen to, houses up, furniture unpacked or freshly pegged together and so on, they began to think of founding a church. But they had been working so hard they really hadn't had time to get to know one another very well, much less talk about what kind of church they should establish. In other words, except that many of them—though not all—were farmers, these folks were something like present day suburbanites, almost all of whom may have moved quite recently to where they now live. Certainly, if suburbanites now think they might want to start a new Unitarian Universalist church, they will have to start by talking with strangers, maybe much like themselves religiously, maybe not, but who certainly do not know each other in any depth.

So, guess what these New Englanders did in 1637 to get to know each other and to approach—gently, slowly—some very profound and personal religious issues, *terra incognita* among them. They set up a series of weekly neighborhood meetings, "lovingly to discourse and consult together . . . and prepare for spiritual communion in a church society, * * * [gap in the record] that we might be further acquainted with the (spiritual) tempers

18

and guifts of one an other." Meetings were held every Thursday "at several houses in order," in rotation. Anybody in town who wanted was welcome to attend.

They adopted a few simple rules for their meetings. Rule 1: They would decide before leaving each meeting what question to discuss next week. That way people were more apt to share *considered* thoughts. Rule 2: Each week the host of the house would begin, speaking to the agreed-upon question. Then everyone else could speak by turns. Each one could, as they chose, speak to the question, or raise a closely related question and speak to that, or state any objections or doubts concerning what any others had said, "so it were humbly & with a teachable hart not with any mind of cavilling or contradicting." In other words, Rule 3 was: Here we speak our own understandings or doubts. No arguing. The record reports that all their "reasonings" were "very peaceable, loving, & tender, much to edification."

Nowadays we seldom say a good meeting contributed to our "edification." Otherwise, what a contemporary ring those rules have! I have sat myself in hundreds of hours of Unitarian Universalist discussion meetings with exactly those rules! Both in a large church of 1000 members, whose members wanted to get to know one another and go to some deep places of the spirit together, which might prove controversial, and in meetings of suburban strangers exploring the possibility of starting a new liberal church together.

The account in the Dedham Church record lists the questions the people in 1637—not yet a church—discussed at their weekly meetings, which continued a whole year, one event really, from the winter season of 1637 until some time after the church was founded in November of 1638. Several features of this event are intriguing. For example, we all know the New England colonists were a "people of the Book," the Bible. But they did not begin to talk about a church by talking about the Bible. By way of laying a basis for discussion of the church, they began by addressing a question of common sense or natural law. I quote, "For the subject of thes disputes or conferences divers meetings att first were spent about questions as pertayned to the just, peaceable & comfortable proceeding in the civill society * * *."

In a word, a foundational concern of a free church is for the justice, the peace, the laws and regulations—the *conditions* of—any healthy, free society. Here in the wilderness these people, having just come from the anguish of European society in the 1600s, knew there could be no peaceably functioning free church—in the long term—if it was not set within a larger society wherein concerns for justice, peace and reasonable laws can be freely and effectively voiced, without suppression. That beginning concern for the conditions of the larger society always remained in the background of the New England free church, and could very readily, at any time, spring to the foreground, if occasion warranted, although the free church certainly had its own more specialized concerns.

At just this point there is an unrecorded assumption in the text of the Dedham Church record, but—I think—if we don't catch the force of it, we are very apt to misread the thrust of much of our own still living past. These New Englanders assumed that the strongest—maybe not the only—but the strongest, clearest, most authentic voice in their whole society—for justice, peace and reasonable laws—would come from the free church, once it was established. Why? Because they understood the divine will of the loving God of the Universe to be for justice, peace and good laws in the whole society. *The* task of the free church could be summed—in their terms—as loving God and loving one another so well that in their own study and discussion, dispute and conference, prayer, consultation and more discussion in the free church, the members might learn together the divine will of the loving God for the whole society insofar as that will relates to justice, peace and reasonable laws. And, if so, the members would be called, compelled, bound to proclaim it and try to bring it to bear in their whole society.

In England, in the decades before the 1630s, there had been no strong, clear, authentic voices for justice, peace and reasonable laws coming from the established State church, as these New Englanders understood things. Furthermore, every effort of laypeople like themselves to get going even quasi-church meetings to discuss such matters—in their homes or in lawyers' professional organizations or in the marketplace—had been systematically thwarted and suppressed. For just such meetings as they were now having in Dedham, people had been fined, jailed, exiled, whipped and even hanged. So, they talked first about the conditions of a good society in general. But the author of the record, John Allin, wrote down no details of their "divers meetings" on this broad subject, perhaps because of the danger that, even out here in the wilderness, 3000 nautical miles from England, a written record could fall into the hands of an unfriendly agent of the king.

Anyhow, after much general talk about "civill society," they began to edge toward talk about a church. Their first question on this subject was: Here we are, not presently members of any church. We don't know each other well, religiously. Are we qualified to "assemble together . . . [and] confer" like this? Their answer: We are if, "in the judgement of charity," we seem to be and think we are acting out of (in our terms) genuinely deep, religious love. I don't want to mislead here. For these Dedham people genuinely deep, religious love meant a union with Christ. I will not till Lecture 3 to get into the details of what they meant by "union with Christ." For now I will just say I am convinced that what they meant by that term generally was no different from what we mean by a phrase like "genuinely deep, religious love."

Next question: Well, if we can meet like this, just as neighbors, isn't this enough? Maybe we don't need a church. Their answer: No, this is too casual. If we really want to live in the ways of our deepest love, then we must intentionally form a much deeper community of love. "The spiritual condition of [even deeply loving people] is such as stand in need of all instituted [helps] for the repaire of the [spirit] and edification of the [whole] body of [the church]." And besides, others in the larger society need the example of love which a free church will publicly show forth. Otherwise, others might not be drawn to the life of effective love, or enjoy the benefits of justice, peace and so on—in "civill society" which the free church will care about and speak out for. My point is that they understood the role of the church as filling needs of both the members and the larger community.

References to the Bible came into their later discussions, precisely when they got into issues of authority inside the church. For they read the Bible with a sociological and political hermeneutic. But what they were doing with reference to Bible stories, is just what I am doing here. They

21

were looking back in time to earlier eras of reform in the records of great free church tradition, to see how things were done back then, and whether those ways made sense to them in their own times.

These laypeople's central conclusion, from all these weeks of discussion, was this: *Members of their new free church should be joined in a covenant of religious loyalty to the spirit of love.* And once the members were joined in a covenant, of their own writing and signing, the members' loyalty in the church should be only to the spirit of love, working in their own hearts and minds. No one—not the Governor, not the General Court, not even members of other similarly covenanted churches—would have any authority in the local free church. They were not sectarian loners. As I shall explain later, they thought they should and they did seek counsel from neighboring churches. Yet they were very careful to make sure everybody understood that they would seek and consider counsel from others often, but accept rulings or commands contrary to their own experience of the spirit—never.

For any who might suppose our 17th-century free-church ancestors talked mostly about original sin, predestination and hellfire, I am glad to be able to tell you, not one of those topics is even mentioned in the record of the founding of the Dedham Church. The document describes these discussions of 1637–38 and the talk, talk, talk at each step of the way to the founding, and on to their first reception of new members after the founding, and on to their first election of officers, after which they ordained two of their own members as pastor and elder.

In these pages there is much use of these words: reason, reasons, reasoned, reasoning, deliberation, make trial of, clearing, cleared up, encouragement, advice, advise, counsel, agree, agreed, agreement, approbation, liberty, liberties and promising. There is also repeated use of the words: sweet, comfort, help and brotherly. But by far the most commonly used words in this written history are: *affection, affections, affectionately, embrace and love, loving, lovingly.* In the first 24 pages I counted 32 uses of the words affection and love. Why? Because then and now and for as long as human history lasts—when all is said and done, done and said some more—*the integrity of the free church comes down to our loyalty to the spirit of love at work in the hearts and minds of the local members.* The laypeople who founded First Church, Dedham knew so and clearly said so, and that is why we still say together, so often in our churches now, "Love is the doctrine of this church. . . ."

May we long continue to say so, and understand deeply what we are saying in the liberal free churches these laypeople founded. In Lecture 2 I shall take up the covenant and ask: How shall we now understand the covenant of the free and liberal church?

Lecture 2:
Thus Do We Covenant

John Allin wrote "a breife history" of the founding of the Dedham First Church into the first 24 pages of its Church Records, Book I. He says in the first paragraph that he wrote this history for us, "for future ages to make use of in any case that may occur wherein light may be fettched from any examples of things past, no way intending hereby to bind the co'science of any to walke by this patterne or to approve of the practise of the Church further than it may appear to be according to the rule of the gospell."

How's that for a liberal understanding of the proper use of any history? Allin says we might learn something useful to us from the example of one of our earliest New England churches. But he wants to be sure we know, he didn't feel we in the 21st century should feel in any way bound to follow our ancestors' example, except insofar as we may find their example correlates with "the gospell," good news for human beings.

What do we count as good news, the "gospell?" Our ancestors used the word Christ as a shorthand term for the life of mutual love. I do not here use that term. Yet, it makes sense to me to believe that if John Allin and other founding members of our New England churches were alive today, they could support this wording: More than any other single reality, *the spirit of mutual love redeems and enhances human life. The good news is: We can learn to recognize the presence of the spirit of mutual love among us. And we can, in response, organize ourselves into a free church, a group religiously dedicated to giving the spirit of love a fine chance of working among us, for our own sakes and for the*

25

sake of the world around us. That's "the gospell," in my book, as I think it was in theirs.

The First Church, Dedham was founded in 1638 by one small group of English colonists from among the 20,000 or so who came here to New England in the 1630s. These 20,000 people came primarily for one reason: They wanted to establish free churches in what they called "the Liberty of the Gospel," in which they could gather for worship, study and discussion as much as they wanted, without the restraint or control of either government or church hierarchies. These ancestors of ours set certain patterns of organization and authority and theology whose consequences are still— very much—alive in our Unitarian Universalist churches.

The marvelous thing about our 17th-century ancestors, in my eyes, is this: *They saw that if the free church is about the working of the spirit of mutual love, then that fact ought to shape the organization of the church, everything from how you join, to what joining means, to how church decisions are made.* Their thinking about the organization of the church didn't just fall down whole out of the sky. "There's no such thing as the immaculate conception of an idea." Their thinking evolved from and in the midst of particular human experience, in England before they left there and in New England after they arrived here. We can't understand their thinking without some empathetic grasp of their experience. So I will try to narrate something of their experience as I describe their thinking.

I ask you to hear me on this: I don't claim these 17th-century ancestors of ours got everything right. I subscribe to the blind-spot theory of human nature, that all of us make mistakes we can't see as mistakes at the time. In fact, I shall say in Lecture 5, our ancestors made some very big mistakes—mistakes still costing us. But I think our understanding of our own beginnings is distorted because we've focused far too singlemindedly on their mistakes. They got some really important institutional patterns right, patterns we need very much to understand and appreciate in order rightly to understand ourselves as people of the free church tradition. Here I will talk about what they got right, which it has been our great privilege to inherit.

I have especially wanted to tell you the story of the founding of the Dedham church for this reason: As far as I know, we don't have any other record, certainly not any other such ample record of the discussions concerning the free church among the laypeople before they established one.

But does the absence of any other such record mean that the laypeople, who founded the other free churches in New England, did not engage in such discussions? Oh, no. All these New Englanders had come out from among and left, back in England, many more thousands much like themselves. In England all these folks had surely been just about the most lay discussion–oriented and the lay talking-est bunch of people in history. Precisely this feature of their character drove the bishops of the Church of England bananas.

We could not here even begin to get into the Reformation going on in Europe—unevenly, sometimes crazily. But to appreciate the kind of free churches from whom ours is descended, you need to know something of what was going on in England in the early 1600s. So, I list just a few facts about the messy social intercourse in England out of which our church founders came.

(1) The law required that everybody attend services in their parish (neighborhood) church every Sunday. (2) Church services in the Church of England then consisted mostly of a lot of old ceremony, which had hardly any meaning for our spiritual ancestors. They considered the services—about which the lay members had no say—dull as dishwater, with ill-educated, ill-trained and poorly-paid assistant ministers (curates) in charge. (3) The Bible had been translated into English. The Bible, of course, is not really a book, but a collection of many little books from many different centuries. And, as more and more laypeople in England got a copy, many of them found the Bible very interesting—and exciting—just full of the neatest stories. (4) Meanwhile also, the professors at Oxford and Cambridge Universities—especially Cambridge—had got very interested in the Bible. Cambridge students were afire with their Bible studies in Hebrew, Greek and English, and with all the new and scholarly Bible commentaries coming off Continental presses. (5) Some ministers—mostly Cambridge graduates—and some Cambridge professors were, then, doing some mighty interesting Bible preaching in some of the churches.

So, tired of the boring services in their own parish churches, the laypeople went gadding. On a Sunday they left their own neighborhoods and went to hear exciting preaching in other parishes. Moreover, they wanted to discuss what they had heard with their neighbors, compare what different preachers had to say with their own interpretations of the stories they had read, themselves. So, the laypeople met in their houses of an evening, with a few other families, for discussion. They met in groups of village and town shopowners—butchers, grocers, hatmakers and so on—and their families. Lawyers met in professional groups for discussion. Sometimes the laypeople even arranged regional meetings, for folks in several neighborhoods to meet and discuss. They were not plotting, or scheming to subvert the Church of England. They just wanted to hear good preaching and talk—and talk and talk and talk—especially since their Cambridge professors had taught them to understand that nearly all the stories in the Bible could be read as having clear political implications with regard to *the liberty of church laypeople.*

Well, the bishops of the Church of England did not take kindly to all this gadding about. Old English phrases stayed in use in the mountains and hills of Appalachia in this country, longer than in many areas. When I was a teen in Louisville, my dad—who was from Appalachia—was always telling me there was just "no use in" my "gadding about" so much. He meant flitting hither and yon, always off somewhere with this or that bunch of friends, without serious purpose. That's still the dictionary definition of gadding. But unlike my dad, who only fussed, the bishops *ordered* the laypeople to stop gadding, to stay home and in the evenings, to stay in their own houses. Any preachers whose sermons the laypeople liked to hear and meet to talk about, the bishops were apt to remove from their pulpits. The bishops also made life as uncomfortable as possible for the Cambridge professors. So, the lawyers and businesspeople, shop owners and craftspeople, established "lectureships" on market days, during the week, outside the churches. On market day, when lots of people came to town, the Cambridge professors would "lecture" to the crowds who wanted to hear them. The bishops shut down these lectureships.

But the bishops didn't get near enough gadding about—and talking—shut down before the laypeople in wide sections of England had worked out, in considerable detail, what a free church would look like, and how authority would be delegated in free churches, the kind of free churches the people had in the Bible stories, without bishops.

But all the English Protestant kings and Queen Elizabeth supported the bishops, and supplied them government agents, to deal as government agents the world over tend to deal with discussion meetings their bosses don't take kindly to. King James I, especially, was always saying, "No bishops, no king." All his royal heirs agreed with James in that. Royal ruler after royal ruler said: Never mind what those people are taking about. Shut 'em down! And if you can catch their leaders, those damned trouble-making ministers, string 'em up! As Defender of the Faith, I appoint the bishops, and the bishops will tell the people what lessons to take from church history as recorded in the Bible.

We might sum the story of our ancestors' experience this way. They came to experience together, more intensely and richly than they ever had before in their lives, the holy spirit of mutual love, in freely organized groups. And that experience led them to conclude, as James Luther Adams used to say, "You can't make the holy spirit work according to an organization chart. 'The spirit bloweth where it listeth.'" Freedom is indispensable to the spirit of love. Try to control it, with a centralized, top-down hierarchical organization, and you will kill it.

Now right here is the point at which the free church tradition in North America begins, as a radically lay-led movement. At some point in the reign of King Charles I—no one knows just how or where—when things got really bad in England for free church wanna-bes, a little group of laypeople—lawyers mostly, with a few wealthy land and business owners—got together to plan a solution. They formed themselves into a new business corporation, called the Massachusetts Bay Company, for which they had to get a charter from the king. By law, if they had a charter from the king to run a business corporation, the officers of the corporate board could run it as they saw fit, as long as they didn't do anything illegal. And members of the governing board of the corporation could both elect their own board governor and change or enlarge the membership of the board. A corporation board was—by law—both self-governing and self-selecting.

Well, these lay lawyers and businessmen got their charter, from King Charles I, and a royal grant of land in North America. (The grant was way bigger than they or the king knew, since nobody in Europe had a clue in the 1600s how big the North American continent was.)

Of course, the Mass Bay Company was really no ordinary corporation. What these lay corporate board members did—and intended all along to do—was to set up a colony, actually an independent government only nominally under the king's jurisdiction, and far enough away from London that English laypeople who wanted could settle in the New England colony and here establish a whole community of free churches, without bishops.

Or, as these laypeople put it, they had a charter—not from the king, but from the Holy Spirit of Love—to gather themselves into corporate bodies of faith, into churches. These laypeople hoped they could, in New England, show, illustrate, demonstrate to all England—to all the world— how just, how peaceful and how comfortably well ordered a society could be if in that society the people were free to found and establish free churches governed by the spirit of mutual love, the kind of free churches there had once been in other long forgotten times of history, when the great free church tradition had been well understood by the laypeople.

Once the new Company had its charter from King Charles, word spread fast in England, but so quietly that it was a few years before the bishops and the king figured out what the people were up to. Not too long after the Company and the people got the colony in North America established, the board of the corporation simply made every man of the churches—and some years later every owner of a piece of land, even a building lot—a member of the Company board, and so eligible to vote in annual elections choosing their governor. By these acts, they made the government of this royal colony, New England, in effect, a proto-democracy.

So, these 20,000 laypeople, by the end of one decade in the 1630s, had planned and pulled off a very clever—and very expensive—legal scheme, indeed. Of course, the very success of their scheme meant they had one hell of a big anxiety-producing problem. For the king had the power to withdraw, at any time and for any reason, the Mass Bay Company's charter. Which fact—even if many things went well—made all life in New England very chancy. The colonists feared—far more than the native Indians—entrance into the Massachusetts Bay of armed English ships, sent by the king's government to seize royal control of their costly experiment. Many had not only left friends and relatives at home, whom they could never hope to see again, in civilized and mostly orderly England, to come out to this wilderness. Many had also risked every shilling they owned. But if he chose, the king could simply declare all deeds to New England property invalid.

And that is why the people of New England were so obsessed with having an orderly, quiet society. They didn't want any scandalous disputes that might end up in the law courts back in England, and thus attract government attention to what was going on over here. That's why they worked so hard to involve many people, for example, in setting up their town councils and forms of representation in the General Court. They wanted laws and regulations everybody could agree on and willingly obey, so that all New England would be—not contentious or argumentative—but orderly and quiet. Not to give the king any excuse for intervention.

And, it makes sense to me to believe, that is also why they so overreacted to Anne Hutchinson. Any doctrine of the church grounded in the holy spirit of love is dangerous. Why? Because always some few—or maybe many—will get the idea that if their heart is in the right place, they can do anything they want, without a lot of tedious reasoning about consequences: Have sex with whomever, just so you're feeling romantic. Get drunk (or take illegal drugs), just so you feel "spiritual release," and so on. Which is not to say Anne Hutchinson advocated this kind of wildness. But back in Europe this had happened. The word "Munster" hung over all church reformers as a threat of doom. Munster was a city in the Netherlands caught up, a century earlier, in 1534, in Protestant enthusiasm. Their devotion to the all-sufficiency of the spirit of Christ—without need of reason or history or laws or good works—turned into an orgy of irrationality, the dictatorship of a talented demagogue, communism and polygamy. Neighboring authorities were outraged. After a long siege, the inhabitants were massacred.

And in England in the early 1600s there were groups who didn't go anything like as far as the Munsterites, but whose personal morals were pretty disorderly. These groups were called "familists." Our New England ancestors meant to protect themselves from the threat of "familism" by structuring their churches so that all religious leaders would be elected, authorized, by established congregations of lay members, and all these leaders would be subject to discipline by the lay members who had elected them and could dismiss them. So, when Anne Hutchinson began attracting a large group of these same lay members—and teaching that if you had Christ in your heart, you didn't need anything else at all—other New Englanders feared their brave experiment would go the way of other reform efforts which had failed disastrously. In their eyes such antinomian teaching was a threat, not only to the colony's good order, but to the community's very survival. That is why they thought they had to expel her when they could not persuade her she was wrong.

And—as if such an outbreak of antinomianism in their own midst were not enough to worry about—the king's ministers all too soon began to request, repeatedly, that the officers of the Mass Bay Company bring that charter back to London. The government had a few questions to ask about it. Over and again, the board of governors "misunderstood" the request—and stalled. They hoped that if they could just get enough fellow religionists still in England to immigrate and build up economically viable farms, towns and businesses, the king would find in politically impossible to dismantle the colony. They feared that if the inevitable government intervention came too soon, the political price of dismantling New England would be one the king could well afford, in which case the colony would not have a political leg to stand on.

Is it any wonder that Governor John Winthrop recorded a sad little story in his journal? One cold winter's night, a good woman awoke to find her good husband sitting bolt upright in their bed. Of course, she asked what was the matter. Without a word in answer, he jumped out of bed and out their bedroom window and took off at a dead run. He was in the throes of what we now now call a full-out anxiety-attack. Out in that bitter cold, in just his nightshirt, the poor man kept running, for hours. The people followed his tracks in the snow. Next morning they found him, 20 miles from home, dead of fear and exhaustion. Now that's anxiety! It makes sense to me to believe that much of the famous religious anxiety recorded in many a New Englander's journal was induced by the political and economic riskiness of their peculiar colonial context. Anxiety was a subtext of every thing they did and every word they wrote.

To me it seems no wonder that New Englanders occasionally went on "witch hunts." Severe and long anxiety, concerning real threats, is itself a threat, to public as well as private sanity.

In the 1640s, civil war in England greatly added to New England's political and especially economic uncertainty. The outcome of the war effectively ended any further immigration for decades. Suffice it to say that at last, their stalling tactics exhausted, the General Court finally delegated the Rev. Increase Mather to take their precious charter and, after a two- or three-month-long sailing trip to England, hand it over to the government of King Charles II. Now, there was absolutely nothing for it but to wait, for months and months and months, while a few individuals—the king and his advisers 3000 miles away—decided their fate. The king chose not to break up this highly irregular social experiment—with its huge number of electors and all those churches uncontrolled by the bishops of the Church of England. But he did take away the colony's right to elect their own governor. Henceforth the colony would clearly be a Royal Colony, with a royally appointed governor.

The hysteria of the Salem witch trials broke out within days of the new Royal Governor's arrival in Boston, not in any of the churches but in a court of law, and rapidly escalated, to the unending shame of all New England. The Rev. Increase Mather's son, the Rev. Cotton Mather, lodged a written protest against the witch trials, but too mildly, too politely for anybody important to notice. After all, it was an anxious time for the Mathers, too. Some blamed Increase Mather for the loss of their charter, and besides that, the new Royal Governor was a member of Increase and Cotton Mather's church. King Charles II had even allowed Increase Mather to nominate New England's first royally appointed governor. Pretty sticky issues here! Imagine the messy politics involved in asking your colonial allies to petition this brand-new Royal Governor to intervene in a bizarre law case, with all that suspicion, distrust and fear in the air! Innocent people died in Salem, as much of other peoples' fear and exhaustion as that lone runner in the night had died of his own. Increase Mather, himself, put an end to the Salem trials with a sermon on convincing and unconvincing evidence. Samuel Sewall, the only judge in Salem to make public confession and annual penitence for his errors in Salem, spent the last years of his life as a frequent attendant of this church in which we are meeting, in Brookline. I wish more of our churches today could welcome more penitents for the deaths we have caused in times of hysterical craziness.

But back to the matter of money in the decade of the 1630s. It took a bunch of money to pay for shipping 20,000 people—as well as their livestock, tools, furniture, seeds and some food—3000 miles across the Atlantic Ocean. But there were plenty of laypeople ready to sell all their possessions to make the trip because they had talked together as laypeople so very much—about the ancient free church tradition and the politics—or polity—of the free church. When they got to New England, especially given all else they had to do, they needed to do very little more talking specifically about how a free church should be set up and governed. They knew, very clearly, what kind of free churches they wanted to found.

(A digression: They did, however, keep up their gadding and talking. They kept their university-educated ministers lecturing, on all sorts of topics, during the week. The laypeople went to one another's churches to hear these late afternoon lectures and often stayed, to talk about the issues raised, into the night. Governor Winthrop decided all these lectures and discussions were taking too much time away from work, and so he moved to suppress them. The laypeople's reaction was swift and to the point. They said: We came 3000 miles across the ocean, Governor, for the liberty of the Gospel, not to have you tell us we do too much gadding about. Governor Winthrop offered a compromise, which the churches accepted. Lectures would mostly be on Thursday afternoons, thereby reducing the gadding. And discussions would, as a "safety precaution," break up in time for people to get home before dark—and up early the next morning to work. Thursday lectures continued in our Unitarian churches until late in the 19th century.)

But by the 1630s, when the New England laypeople first got here, most of them didn't need the kind of discussions, specifically about the free church, which they had in Dedham. When most of them settled here in a new neighborhood, they had been gadding about in the same neighborhoods in England, attending the same market-day "lectures," sharing in the same regional meetings, and talking, talking, talking, about the right ordering of free churches, for years. And that is doubtless why we have no records of their discussions on the matter, here.

Dedham settlers, however, did not know one another. These laypeople had come from "divers parts" of England, and wanting to be sure they were agreed on so important a matter, they felt they had better talk through the whole idea of the free church, very slowly and thoroughly. But you couldn't ask for stronger proof than the Dedham Church, itself, that the Dedham lay discussions—in their year of weekly meetings—were quite characteristic of the many, many earlier lay discussions which had already taken place in England. For the Dedham Church, once it was independently founded, fit the organizational pattern—the covenantal pattern—of all the New England churches of the period, to a tee.

The *covenantal organizational pattern* of the free church was the key element of our ancestor's doctrine of the free church. It is a doctrine grounded in an understanding of how the power of mutual love deepens and works among individuals in free religious groups—that is, in free religious groups loyal, before all else, to the spirit of love. Moreover, their organizational pattern is precisely the one element of our ancestors' doctrine we liberals have most consistently kept in our liberal free churches. It's a remarkable thing that this should be true. Many liberals, by the early 19th century, had forgot the originating meaning of the word covenant. And by the mid-20th century, many if not most liberals had all but completely forgotten where we got the organizational pattern of our free churches, and had forgotten—as the Little Valley Church did—that no free church organization can work very well if it is not consciously, explicitly grounded in the spirit of love.

Here's how I first realized how much we have forgotten. The term we now use for covenantal free church organization is congregational polity. As a seminary student, I had got really excited upon learning, for the first time, about the theological origins of congregational polity, way back there on the radical left wing of the Reformation in the 17th century. I was talking with my own UU minister, a wonderful, able minister, who had himself grown up in not a UU but another congregational church. He listened to me emote and effuse a while, and then he said, "Congregational polity: That means our churches are democratic. But what does that have to do with our religion?"

I was dumbfounded. I could not say one word. In a way, you could say, I am trying now, nearly 30 years later, to answer that question. In one sentence, it has *everything* to do with what we hold, even if unconsciously, to be most important religiously. Here is a one-sentence summary of the lay doctrine of the free church as it was developed by laypeople, our institutional ancestors, in the 17th century: *Show me the patterns of your church organization, and I'll show you what the people of the church find worthiest of their loyalty as churchpeople.* Organization and theology are not two different things. Our organization is a function of our actual theology.

The patterns of thought and action visible in the story of the Dedham Church's founding, their lived teaching, their doctrine of the free church: Here I'll list eight of these patterns, though the list does not yet include all of them. There are other patterns of the free church—very important ones, some of which our ancestors not long after the 1630s and in the 19th century got wrong. I'll speak of these in Lecture 5. But for now, these are eight key patterns which—I believe—our Dedham ancestors and others, at the beginning of our North American free church tradition, got so very importantly right.

(1) Right at the heart of a free church must be the *spirit of love*. The free church is a group of people who want the spirit of love to reign in their lives. To quote the Dedham Church record, the desire for a "further & neerer union & communion" of love they conceived to be the one good reason for founding a free church, or for joining one already founded. It still is.

(2) The free church is entirely *self-governing*, free from any outside control whatsoever. Whatever obligations members may honor outside the church—to governments, to the larger community, to family duties, bosses at work, whatever—these have no authority in the church. Local members elect their own officers—ministerial and lay—and by their decisions govern every facet of their local church community's life.

(3) Loyalty to the spirit of love simultaneously commits members of

36

the free church to *the best understanding of truth we can attain*, and that means reasoning. Precisely because they loved, the laypeople of New England wanted to reason well about truth and about facts. That is why a learned ministry was so important to them. They did not elevate their ministers because of their learning. Rather, they figured if a learned minister spoke the truth plainly, it would convince them. That is why they often listened to a prospective new minister for months, and discussed and discussed every aspect of his addresses before they agreed to elect him. And of course, the laypeople kept for themselves the power to dismiss any elected officer—ministerial or lay—if a lot of high-sounding words proved meaningless to them.

(4) *Reasoning together about what we love*, and about all the social implications and complexities of love, in continuous consultation, has been a built-in part from the very beginning of the free church tradition from which we Unitarian Universalists have come. Continuous consultation our ancestors called "walking together." Herein lies the free-church concept of discipline. If any member's actions, or his or her attitude—"carriage," our ancestors called it—if any member's "carriage" seemed scornful or sarcastic or sullen or ungenerous, he or she would likely be called upon the next afternoon by the Elder to "cleer" things. Members of the free church *discipline one another by reasoning together in love*, whenever any members see it as needed. Not long ago on the UUMA e-mail chat list, one of our newer ministers was asked to define discipline in the free church. I think he gave a wonderful answer. He said discipline in the free church is *forbearance and engagement*. No member of a free church is "cast out" for dissent on some proposition. Rather, a persistent refusal to engage with forbearance is the only proper cause for removing any member from the roll.

(5) *Membership in the free church is open to individuals willing to sign a covenant—or promise—to be together, insofar as they are able, as a beloved community.* The covenant summarizes, in clear and simple language, an understanding of points 1, 2, 3 and 4. And that the authentic free church is always covenanted means two other things.

(6) The free church is an organized, not an organic, group. You're not a member just because you happened to be born in the parish and your

37

parents brought you up in the church. No. *The covenanted free church is an organization you must freely choose individually to join.*

(7) When you sign the membership book of a covenanted free church, you are not signing any list of propositions, such as make up a creed: "I believe this, that, the other and maybe forty-'leven other things." No. To join a free church is to sign a promise that may sound simple—it should sound simple—but which, if you "keep covenant," *brings you into intimate companionship with others who have promised to live with all the integrity you and they can together muster,* in all the years of your lives.

No simple matter this. Entrance into the covenantal community summons a lifelong, forbearing engagement of heart, mind and body. So why would anybody ever rejoice to sign such a promise and regard it as a great privilege to do so? Because we human beings, social creatures through and through, are gifted individually—such is the dignity of human nature—to experience and to learn and to claim as our own these wonderful truths: *Ultimately, the only freedom adequate to human dignity is the freedom to do what love asks of us. And the greatest blessings of life come to us and through us to all the world when, with intimate and freely bonded companions, we are trying together to live with the integrity of faithful love.* All this is what it means to say together in our church:

> Love is the doctrine of this church,
> The quest of truth is its sacrament,
> And service is its prayer.
> To dwell together in peace
> To seek knowledge in freedom,
> To serve human need,
> To the end that all souls shall grow into harmony with
>   the Divine—
> Thus do we covenant with each other and with God.

(8) Still another characteristic of the most basic pattern of thinking about the doctrine of the free church is there in the record of the Dedham laypeoples' discussion. I mean the large place given—in the earliest thinking of our New England beginnings—to *natural law.* That is, to thinking about, insofar as we are able, *what faithfulness to the ways of love*

means to the whole human race and world. I related in Lecture 1 how the Dedham laypeople started their discussions by considering the conditions requisite, in any society, for justice, peace and reasonable laws—"comfortable proceedings," they called them. But also, even when the Dedham laypeople began to talk about the covenant, the basic document of the church they would later compose and sign, they first cited a natural-law argument for such a covenant. "The ground of which covenant was shewed from the nature of the thing * * * being no union of many p'sons into one body that can be made without mutuall consent or some kind of covenant."

Then, "2ly," they went on to cite from history, from the Bible, "the stories of Abraha' & his family constituted a church by covenant Gen 15 & 17. the people of Israel coming out of Egypt Exod: 20 &c. & when thei brak that covenant this caused ther divorce from the lord, & when they were restored againe in any way of solemn reformation it was by renewing this covenant as many examples shew." Then, "3ly," they cited five passages in the New Testament which they took to indicate clearly, or to imply clearly, that the earliest Christian churches were "such as agree together" in a covenant.

I want to say this carefully. I do not mean to say or even to suggest that our New England ancestors did not hold the Bible to be a book of "special" revelation. I say only this: The word revelation is not mentioned in the *Dedham Church Records*, Book I. Moreover, the whole structure of the argument in these discussions is one in which *common sense or natural law and the Bible are taken to be entirely compatible.* There is no talk recorded of any miracles or anything else hard to believe—except how strangely and wonderfully love works. Love deepens in committed, religious relationships in the free church. Deep love and careful, social, shared reasoning in the church evokes deep loyalty to love's end, which is *meaningful freedom*, freedom within boundaries defined by a high degree of tender caring and within which all are fully included, as equals. Once the Dedham Church was founded and the founding members were ready to accept new members, they were joined by servants and the richest people in their town, by young apprentices and the very aged, by people of all occupations, by women and men. No matter what their status in civil society, in

39

the church all members took part in their discussions and each member had one vote.

Our ancestors in this church believed that the laypeople in one ancient land had been inspired—or had learned—or invented—however you want to put it—laypeople in one ancient land had embraced the covenant of the free church which fits so well the very nature of human beings as individuals and as the social creatures we all are, that once you grasp the idea—of the spirit of love which may reign in a free church of equal members—the truth of it will naturally appear to you as self-evident. More, taken together in all its strands and lived, *the covenanted free church is the best hope of the world.*

The laypeople of Dedham in 1637–38 did not know, and had no way of knowing, that a few non-Judaic-Christian peoples had also embraced the idea of the covenant. People in ancient Switzerland, for example, and the Iroquois among the Native Americans on this continent have been covenanted peoples, among others. The laypeople of Dedham in 1637–38 *did* know that the covenantal idea cannot be taken for granted as something "once and for all delivered to the saints," so that good people can set that notion aside and go on to other things. On the contrary, the laypeople of Dedham understood that *the covenantal idea of the free church has been nearly lost many times, and the results of the loss have always been political tyranny and corruption.* The idea of the free church has to be articulated in clear, fresh language and taught and lived, if the free church is to live, and the freedom of whole societies with it. In Lectures 3 and 5 I shall try to make sense of our later church history, to suggest why and how we Unitarian Universalists came close to losing it.

But I want to turn now to our present. How might we come to a wide lay understanding of the idea of the covenant in our churches now, and embrace one another in our own contemporary covenants, specially written by the members of our churches, for our churches? Then I'll come back to the free-church covenants of New England in the 1600s, and say a bit more of them.

In our time our liberal Unitarian Universalist churches are not only quite diverse theologically, as we want, on principle, to be. It would not occur to most of our people to look in the Bible to see what we might want to promise each other in a church covenant. And even if we did, we probably would not see, without a lot of help from some liberation theologians, the *political* meanings of biblical history, which our ancestors learned from their Cambridge scholars to read from it. We live now in very different political times than those of 17th-century England. The Rev. David Johnson, minister of our Brookline Church, could tell us true and horrible 20th-century stories about government infiltration of church activities. But, in general, government agents do not now come banging on our doors to break up church discussion meetings. Nor do we have laws requiring everybody to attend Sunday services. All of which means that any discussions we might have among laypeople in our churches now—in the hope that these might lead to the writing of a church covenant—would need to have a very different starting-point from the 1637–38 discussions of the Dedham laypeople.

Even so, our times *are* like those of the 17th century in important ways. People who show up at our services—many of them—sure have been doing a lot of gadding about, popping in and out of all kinds of religious and other social groups, looking for what? Not finding what? Still looking for what? Why are people in our time so dissatisfied and socially volatile?

Anxieties in our times do not have the same sources as those of 17th-century New England, and yet, anxiety is anxiety. We are not now—since the fall of the USSR—so afraid that nuclear bombs might end our whole world, though we do fear terrorist attacks. Nor do most of us worry that we might lose every dollar we own, though we might lose our jobs to downsizing. We could probably get another job, maybe a better one.

It makes sense to me to believe this: In our time a major source of anxiety is that *we don't know what matters most to us, what we love most*. Many don't know what might be worthy of our faithful loyalty, which people might deserve our trust, or who are the people—or causes or institutions—to whom we might want to be faithful. So I would like to describe a year-long series of discussions that laypeople in our time might find wonderfully "edifying," orienting us toward a new or renewed covenant of a liberal free church, today.

41

In this proposed discussion series there are only two questions, each with many answers, and then, finally, a third. Each person in a group of— say—20 or 25 is given a sheet of paper, blank except for the heading: *The realities of my life to which or to whom I really want to be loyal or faithful.*

To help us get started, we might post a list of realities to which some might want to be faithful: my children's education; my aged parents; my life mate or partner; my ideal of an informed citizenry; my career; a field of study, literature, science or music; economic justice for minorities; my church community; God—or that which I hold sacred or holy; honesty and commonsense; my physical or emotional health. . . . The list is not meant to be in any way exhaustive, only suggestive of the kind of realities people might want to list for themselves.

Rules for our discussion would need to be very like those of the Dedham laypeople. Rule 1: We'll decide each week which one or two people will speak next week, so that we come having considered what we want to say. Rule 2: We stick to our agenda and don't allow ourselves to get off-track talking about other matters. And Rule 3: Here we speak our own understandings and doubts. No arguing.

Then, in the weeks following, each person, one at a time, would share his or her list and try to tell others *why* and *how* he or she wants to be faithful to these realities. Everybody else would then be invited, exercising the discipline of forbearing engagement, gently to ask the speaker for clarification, or to cite different or varied loyalties of his or her own in a particular regard, and so on, always without argument.

When all have asked any questions they wish, or shared with the evening's speaker whatever variations or differences in their own lives they wish, then the group would need to discuss a second question: How could we help a person wanting to be faithful in the ways Person X has spoken of? All who wish may speak to the question, or make personal demurrals to what others say, such as, "I'm not sure that would help to me. I think I would want another kind of help."

When each has spoken about his or her own list, then we might go round again, to see whether, having listened to all this discussion, some may want to emend their lists: "I see that I left off something important." Or, "I now have a rather different list from when we started talking." A second go-round, with observance of the same rules as before, would probably take quite a bit less time than the first, but take us deeper into what matters most to us.

At this point, then, we might move the discussion to the level of natural law. We could make one list of all the realities to which—or to whom—this one group of liberal church people really wants to be loyal or faithful. Then we could try to think about how these religious commitments would play out in the larger neighborhood or society. Our third question: If everybody in a society were faithful to these realities, would this be a civil society of "just, peaceable & comfortable proceeding?" Whose need for mutual love would be left out; whose would be met?

Would these be deeply religious discussions, having to do with the realities of our lives worthiest of our love? And of the loyalty deep love asks of us? I think so. I think very much so. These discussions would help us to get to know one another very well, and lay the appropriate groundwork for meetings to follow, designed to elicit the writing, or the renewal, of our own liberal free-church covenant. What would a new covenant look like, written by and signed by all the members, constituting a free and liberal congregation of Unitarian Universalists of our times? How would it be worded? I like very much this adaptation of the Pilgrims' covenant:

> We pledge to walk together in the ways of truth and
> affection
> as best we understand them now or may learn them in
> days to come
> that we and our children might be fulfilled
> and that we might speak to the world in words and
> actions
> of peace and good will.

At issue is: What covenant or promise might our members enter gladly, after a long and slow, exceedingly loving and gentle and disciplined conversation about our deepest loves?

Most of our oldest Unitarian Unitarian churches—those of our founders in the 1630s in New England—were gathered as signatories of very short covenants, promises of a few words. Unfortunately for the purposes of a neat narrative, the Dedham Church had a very long covenant, too long to include here. The covenant of the Salem Church, written in 1629, is a good example of others very like it. "We Covenant with the Lord and one with an other; and doe bynd our selves in the presence of God, to walke together in all his waies, according as he is pleased to reveale himself unto us in his Blessed word of truth."

The radical thrust of the Salem covenant is given voice especially in two words, "unto us." They granted ultimate religious authority solely to that convincing power of truth evident in the understandings reached and tested over time by a body of *deeply loving* individuals *mutually pledged* faithfully to seek and to heed truth together, in ongoing community, so long as their earthly life should last.

However we, after much discussion, might write our covenants, in liberal free churches today, I am sure the words we choose would make it quite obvious: We belong to and at our best want passionately to be loyal to our long free-church tradition and to keep it live and strong in our time.

Lecture 3: How We Came to Forget the Covenant for a Long Time

> Love is the doctrine of this church . . .
> To dwell together in peace,
> To seek knowledge in freedom.
> To serve human need . . .
> Thus do we covenant with each other and with God.

We often read these lines in our services. Lovely and concise, they give voice to our historic doctrine of the free church. They give voice to what is at once finest and oldest in our nearly 400 years of North American Unitarian Universalist institutional history. Here is a brief account of our beginnings, which I spelled out at some length in Lectures 1 and 2.

In the late 16th and early 17th centuries, certain widespread groups in England, on the far-left wing of the Protestant Reformation, radically reconceived the organization of the church. These people belonged to, but were very critical of, the Church of England. They were highly sociable and highly literate people, of all economic classes, though largely of the new and "rising" middle class. Among them were many university professors, many university-educated preachers and many tens of thousands of laypeople. I am talking about the English Puritans. They hated that name and did not themselves use it. They just called themselves Christians or—eventually—congregationalists.

These radical ancestors of ours said, we know—we experience— God as *the spirit of mutual love*. This reality alone is worthy of our utmost

45

loyalty, our religious loyalty. Quoting scripture, they said, "The spirit bloweth where it listeth." Or, as Prof. James Luther Adams used to paraphrase their doctrine, "You can't make the holy spirit work according to an organization chart." That is to say, an understanding of what religious love requires of us does not flow from archbishop to bishops, to parish ministers, to the flocks in the pews.

Rather, said they, authentic churches are constituted by their members' entry into a covenant—or promise—faithfully to walk together in the spirit of mutual love. They said, members of any local church, gathered in heartfelt union with the holy spirit of love, can discern together whither the spirit leads. Therefore, the most authentic church has no head but the holy spirit of love, or Christ. Their radical doctrine relocated religious authority in the lived spirit among covenanted members. Thus they denied authority to all forms of hierarchical government or ecclesiastical control of churches. In "the liberty of the gospel" members would obey in the church, not king or bishop but only the direction of the holy spirit working in their own hearts and minds.

That is the nub, by no means all, but the essence of what we have come to call the doctrine of congregational polity. We would, I think, better call it the doctrine of *covenantal* church organization.

Over the course of the 1630s—a decade—there occurred the Great Migration. Some 20,000 people crossed the Atlantic to establish, in the New England wilderness, a whole community of covenanted free churches. For some 200 years—until the early 1800s—these churches were identified, not by any "denominational" name, but simply as "churches of the Standing Order." The oldest churches of our UU Association were churches of the Standing Order. That is, our congregations were among those established in the 1630s and somewhat later, as settlements spread from the Massachusetts Bay into the Connecticut Valley and beyond. (Our churches in Plymouth and Salem, MA were established in 1620 and 1629.)

Over the course of the 1700s—a century—many of these same churches slowly, and with relatively little controversy, became first Arminian in their anthropology (the nature of human nature) and then unitarian in their theology of God. Around 1805 the theology of God and anthropology did become matters of heated and divisive debate all over New England. As a result of this long debate—known as the Unitarian Controversy—our New England churches, already long unitarian, came in the 1800s to be *named* Unitarian.

Here is the feature of that history I want us to understand. Not a part of the Unitarian Controversy at all, was the institutional side of our church life: the authority of the members, of each independent congregation, together to write their own covenant, to elect and ordain their own ministers and to govern their churches in all ways. *Unitarian Churches uniformly and unanimously kept the doctrine of congregational polity, or covenantal organization, inherited from our 17th-century founders.* Still today all our member congregations of the Unitarian Universalist Association of Congregations (UUA) are organized in accordance with it. In Lecture 2 I listed eight elements of our founders' doctrine of the church.

Still another feature of any doctrine of the church has to do with authentic patterns of cooperation *among* churches. If a free congregation is a body of persons covenanted to walk together in love, must there not also be *a covenant of the churches* to walk together in love as churches, so that no congregation becomes only local—that is, too parochial in its concerns or too isolated to be helped in time of trouble? How ought free churches be related so that they can help one another?

I need clearly to say here: This feature of our liberal doctrine of the church is muddled and has long been muddled. And I am driving toward a discussion of reform in just this aspect of our doctrine and practice in Lectures 5 and 6. But, I hold, to understand how we came to have such historically weak patterns of cooperation among our churches, we need also to understand how those disputes over anthropology and the theology of God evolved as they did in the Unitarian Controversy. So, in this Lecture 3 I will deal with these matters as well.

I need also to note here that Unitarian and Universalist congregations were not institutionally linked until the UUA was organized in 1961. (They earlier explored the possibilities of union and earlier cooperated in some limited ways.) In the time I have, I cannot even touch on the institutional history of our Universalist churches. Yet I think no Universalist historian would contradict me in this. Whatever Unitarian or Universalist period you want to talk about, you could well say this: However fine our churches have been, internally or out in the world, never have our churches been noted for the fine ways we cooperate with one another. A recent UUA president has said trying to get our churches to work together is "like herding cats." Many a Unitarian and Universalist leader of the past 200 years would sigh from their graves, "Ah, yes. 'Like herding cats!'"

Human history is full of anomalies. This one, so patent among us, I want us to deal with. The 17th-century articulation and practice of the (then) radical covenantal doctrine of the free church preceded and led to secular doctrines of political freedom, to the constitutional and democratic government of free states. Two historic political documents, *The Fundamental Orders of Connecticut* of 1639 and *The Massachusetts Body of Liberties* of 1641, written and adopted by our earliest church founders, served as models for the U.S. Constitution. In both, you can see the doctrine of congregational governance carried over and applied to civil government. The covenantal doctrine of the church changed—and is still changing—the course of world history. Yet, for a long stretch of time, the liberal doctrine of church governance received oddly little attention among us. In much of the 20th century we almost forgot the word covenant.

In 1988 the Rev. Judith Walker-Riggs addressed a colloquium on theology at a General Assembly. She said, "You won't find congregational polity indexed in [the works of]. . . ." And she reeled off a string of scholars' names. "It is not mentioned in any of the articles about us in the Encyclopedias of Religion, and good UUs wrote those articles."

It is only fair to add that Unitarian Prof. James Luther Adams long taught a course at Harvard Divinity School to our seminary students on the Radical Left Wing of the Reformation. Conrad Wright, Harvard professor of church history (now emeritus), has told us in his books that, at its best, congregational polity—or covenantal organization—is the doctrine of a community of independent churches, not of independent churches in uncooperative isolation. And recently, in response to the work of a Commission, some leaders of our Association have been trying to get us to engage in a re-covenanting process. Some groups have done so. But it's an uphill struggle because, as a people, we have forgot the history of our own practices.

I earlier quoted JLA saying, "There is no such thing as the immaculate conception of an idea." All ideas are born of messy social intercourse. All ideas bear the marks of concrete events, which happened within and/or against the social structures of particular times. Now I want to say the same of forgetfulness. Ideas are not just lost to consciousness in a fit of absent-mindedness. Social unawareness—of how and why we ever started doing things as we do—is the fruit of concrete events.

So, in this effort of mine to help us retrieve and reformulate our doctrine of the liberal church, I mean to sketch—not a full or definitive but—a plausible answer to the question: *Why, given our history, are UU churches so uncooperative?* To do that I will have to go back again to ideas and events of the 1600s and move forward.

Cooperation among our earliest churches

Cooperation among churches of the Standing Order was, on theological grounds, never routine. But there was a great deal of it. In 1637 founders of the Dedham Church, for example, spent a year meeting to decide how to establish their church. They made all their own decisions. But they several times sent one or two leaders to ask of another church, What do you think of so-and-so? or, What did you do about this-or-that?

Also, from the beginning and for a good 250 years, there were many, many informally arranged pulpit exchanges. The ministers very often preached in other pulpits than their own. In the mid-1800s, Henry David Thoreau wrote in *A Week on the Concord and Merrimack Rivers* of the "Monday men" going home after pulpit exchanges, "They cross each other's routes all the country over like warp and woof, making a garment of loose texture. . . ."

Lay members, too, wove the institutional "garment" with their travels. They went to Thursday lectures in other churches than their own, and these were often followed by hours of discussion. Lay members also attended Sunday services—morning and afternoon—when they visited friends, as they often did for a week or even a season.

More formally, when members of a local church were unable to resolve some difference, they asked for a council meeting. On an appointed day, neighboring parishes each sent leaders, lay and ordained, to meet with the troubled church and hear all sides of the dispute. The council then offered non-binding advice, most often accepted. And, on rare occasions, church leaders met in formal synods. Conclusions of a synod, like those of the councils, were advisory only, until members of a local church voted to adopt them in their own meeting.

Thus, with no hierarchy, but with a number of well-used *lateral* patterns of engagement, the churches influenced and helped each other substantially for some 200 years. These institutional patterns, by their very design, both allowed scrupulous respect for each congregation's independence and encouraged effective cooperation. On the whole they did both, quite well.

Even so, events began very early to complicate and weaken these patterns. To grasp their consequences, which still today ricochet around our movement, I think we have to try to grasp the spiritual experience our founders thought should be—had to be—at the heart of a covenanted church. I spoke of it a few minutes ago as "heartfelt union with the holy spirit of love." What did that phrase mean in our earliest churches? I explain it this way.

Salvation as ecstasy, or something more sedate?

The generation that founded our churches came to New England with what I will call a "Cinderella" concept of salvation. Every soul, they held, is, like Cinderella, born into a very low estate she is powerless to change, but from which she may be rescued by the power of divine mutual love.

The role of the Puritan preacher was akin to that of Cinderella's fairy godmother. His task was, with his preaching, to make Cinderella understand her ashy condition—that is, the hatefulness of her sinful state. But the preacher also made it possible for her to "go to the royal ball" and see the splendid life of the palace. The sermon, praising the glory of Christ, could arrange for the soul to "look in on" a far different and better life, as a stranger, an outsider unworthy of such a company. If she thus beheld Christ the Prince of Peace, she might fall in love with him and, therefore, earnestly mourn her low estate—her sinfulness—the more.

All the members of the church were also "Cinderellas," but they had already experienced the story. So they knew that if the plot goes forward, as it may, once any soul has been rightly humbled of heart, the Prince himself might, some time, suddenly appear directly to Cinderella. In the fairy tale the prince was able to find her because of the glass slipper business. In our forebears' story, the Prince had chosen her for his own before the foundation of the world. Indeed, distress over her sinful state was a hopeful sign that he had chosen her, that his prevenient grace was already working to ready her for transformation.

The salient point is the splendor, the ecstasy, of their union. In an extraordinary and exalted moment, the Prince/Christ appeared to the individual soul directly, declared his love for that one person and claimed him or her as his bride. They married, and she or he was in union with the holy spirit of love, henceforth no stranger, but from that day a member of the royal household, the kingdom of God.

Now, as the old saying has it, the course of true love never runs smooth. Or, as we say now, good relationships take a lot of hard work, and growth in our relationships can be very painful. Members of Puritan churches did not expect their spiritual lives to be all ecstasy, anything but. Yet the experience of ecstatically transforming and sustaining religious love, our forebears understood as the normal and normative experience of members of the church, all of whom were, individually and corporately, the Bride of Christ. The covenant of the individual soul with Christ was a mutual bond of spiritual marriage, a union of love. The covenant of members with one another was, likewise, a binding mutual promise to walk together as a people loyal, before all else, to the holy spirit of love.

I have used this "Cinderella" language as a shortcut. My aim is to communicate an accurate sense of our ancestors' spirituality. In our culture now, the pains and the ecstasy of "falling in love" are constantly celebrated in our popular art.

> Some enchanted evening you may see a stranger,
> You may see a stranger across a crowded room. . . .

If we've ever hummed along with those lyrics—or many others— we can be empathetic with our founders' religious experience of "falling in love."

Here are some sample quotations, such as can be picked almost at random from early 17th-century Puritan sermons. This one is from *The Golden Sceptre: 6 Sermons on II Chron. 7: 14*, by John Preston, Cambridge professor, for a time court chaplain of Charles I, and "lecturer" to an association of London lawyers, in 1625:

> . . . God the Father gives Christ to us, as a father gives his son as a husband to one in marriage. . . . A man [should say in his heart], . . . that "all within the compass of this world is mine, (a great dowry), that Paul, . . . and all the good ministers that ever have been, have been for my sake. . . ." When therefore your eyes are opened to the Lord himself, you will see such things in him as will make you fall in love with him.

Here is Thomas Hooker, who had much to do with the *Fundamental Orders of Connecticut*, preaching, in 1629:

> Were it not a wonderful great folly if some great king should make love to a poor milkmaid, and she should put it off and refuse the match till she were a queen; whereas, if she will match with the king, he will make her a queen afterwards. So we must not look for sanctification [a raised spiritual estate] till we come to the Lord in vocation; for this is all the Lord requires of thee: to see thy sins and be weary of them. . . . [*The Poor Doubting Christian Drawn to Christ*]

Peter Bulkley was the first minister of our church in Concord, MA. These lines are from his book, *The Gospel Covenant*, published in 1651:

> [W]hen the mighty God of heaven and earth takes his people into the covenant with him, he is a husband to them, and marries them to himself. . . . As a woman may say of him to whom she is married, this man is my husband; and so may every faithful soul say of the Lord, he is my God.

The bridal metaphor was by no means the only one in our founding preachers' quiver. They used as great a wealth of rhetorical figures of speech as did Shakespeare. But the bridal metaphor is everywhere in the Puritan sermonic literature of the 17th century. It provides our best clue for understanding their doctrine of *preparation*.

Think of the emotional stages of the Cinderella story, as she passed through fear, humiliation, doubt, hopeful anticipation, the pleasure of being at the ball, followed by despair in face of her future. As these emotional stages are necessary to the plot of the Cinderella story, our ancestors believed similar spiritual stages must necessarily prepare every soul for the climactic moment of ecstatic spiritual union. Historian Harry Stout says sermon series often dealt, one at a time, with the stages of preparation for grace, and congregations loved these sermons. No wonder! They were about the most intimate and important experience of their lives, of which they never could tire of hearing.

Even so, there early occurred a development very puzzling and alarming to members. Before all the first generation had died, membership in the churches began to decline. Young adults of the second generation were not joining. Something had to be done. But what? Leaders came up with a solution called the Half-Way Covenant. First proposed in 1657 and adopted by a synod in 1662, it was never adopted by all the churches. Our Dedham Church refused and later adopted it two or three times. The Half-Way Covenant, I say, marks the beginning of a long, twisty, windy path of historical developments in which the covenant began to lose its clear meaning as the mutual bond of love which constitutes the free church and determines the shape of its organization.

The issue in the 1650s and '60s came down to the primacy of ecstatic religious experience. Young adults were not applying to sign the covenant because they had had no ecstatic religious experience. And, since the church only baptized children of covenanted members, their babies could not be baptized and, so, had no claim on the care and nurture of the church. Two things here were unthinkable: (1) that ecstasy might not be a primary experience for every soul; and (2) that the founders' grandchildren should be denied the baptismal "seal" of belonging in God's covenant with his people. As a way out of their dilemma, those churches approving the Half-Way Covenant, in effect, agreed temporarily to bracket ecstasy. God had said to Abraham,

> I will establish my covenant between me and you, and
> your offspring after you throughout their generations, for
> an everlasting covenant, to be God to you and to your off-
> spring. [Gen. 17: 7]

Our founders reasoned that since their covenant with God was the same as Abraham's, surely God's spirit would, sometime, come personally upon their children. Was that not, in fact, guaranteed? So, if grown-ups had been baptized in and brought up in the church, and if they were of upright, not "scandalous" life, then they could be admitted to membership before—not exactly without but *before*—an ecstatic, transforming experience, and their children could be baptized.

The stilted, rambling style, of the report recommending the Half-Way Covenant, could be taken as evidence that even its proponents knew it was not very good theology. A covenant is a vow of faithful love. But their solution fuzzed the difference between a covenant of love and a contract to perform certain narrowly prescribed acts, as though the "Bride of Christ" should say, "Well, our 'husband' did contract to carry out the household trash. And our trash is rather piling up, unremoved. But he will get around to it, one day. Anyway, our very own trash is not so offensive. We can live with it."

As a liberal I say, the problem was with their mistaken notion that the path to an authentic religious life of love must include ecstasy. The religious life of many splendidly loving people—and churches—is much more sedate. Members in the 1650s might have entered into a conversation with the young people. "Let us tell you what we mean by promising, as best we can, to be a community faithful to the spirit of love. If what we say makes sense to you and if you, too, yearn for life in a holy community, we invite you to join with us in the covenantal way." That, in fact, is just what we ought to say, in our own words, to people thinking of joining our churches today.

But they couldn't utter such a simple message, because they thought authenticity had to involve ecstasy. Oddly, the Dedham folks had readily exercised "the judgement of charity" in welcoming all who would to take part in discussions that led to the founding of their church. But, though their beloved minister tried hard to persuade them otherwise, these same lay members believed "charity" could not be a criterion in admitting their own children to the church once it was founded!

There were at least three very sad, long-term consequences of confusion over what is required for entrance into the church's covenant:

(1) Over time, the whole idea of the covenant got all tangled up with the notion of a divine contract with all New England and with the hopeful Judaic-Christian doctrine of history. Some became convinced the "signs" pointed to the imminent "Second Coming" and realization of the kingdom of God on earth in America. Thus "federal theology"—as it was called from the Latin word for covenant, *foedus*—became so convoluted and embarrassing that the covenant tended to slide out of liberal discourse.

(2) Without clear emphasis on what it meant to sign the covenant, over time and in practice, though never in theory, membership in the Standing Order churches gradually became far more a matter of family connections—genetic inheritance—than a deliberate religious choice. By the 1800s all of New England's old congregational churches, including the Unitarians', were ethnic churches, as much so as those of Boston's— by then many—Irish Roman Catholics.

(3) All the old congregational churches, conservative and liberal, before and after separation, were repeatedly set a-roil and swamped with conflict generated by folks who just couldn't affirm a religious life without a metaphysically conceived, transcendent ecstasy, unlike anything else in everyday life. In the conservative camp, the troublemakers were the revivalists of the First and Second "Great Awakenings." On our side they were the "Transcendentalists." If I were to read you the diary accounts of their conversion experiences, written by the revivalist Jonathan Edwards and by Transcendentalist Henry David Thoreau, you wouldn't be able to guess who wrote which.

But let's get back to those young adults of the second generation in the 17th-century churches. Why weren't they joining? This account makes sense to me: The imagery of the "Cinderella" concept of salvation reflects the pyramidal class structure of pre-modern European society. In that society the kings and princes, archbishops and so on were way up there on the narrow top, the nobility on tiers a little lower, small property owners below them, and the great mass of the population way down on "Cinderella's" level. The first generation of New Englanders knew that pyramidal structure first-hand. That fact made the imagery of salvation from a very low *spiritual* estate accessible to them. Their children knew no such extremes of class difference. Marked difference, yes; extreme difference, no. And that is one reason Puritan preaching so rapidly declined in its effectiveness in New England. New England class structure provided no objective correlative to the low spiritual estate the Puritan preachers addressed. Therefore, over time, especially young hearers were increasingly less inclined to see their natural spiritual estate as so low as all that!

At the same time, young hearers growing up under such preaching heard constantly that their most intimate and personal feelings were of cosmic importance. So, some concluded, if they didn't *feel* themselves to be of such low estate, then they were *not* of such low estate. Nor need they worry about their spiritual lives just because they never were religiously swept off their feet.

I do not mean that class issues are always the major factor in people's theology. I am saying lived doctrines of spiritual health are always linked to many features of our lives. And I am saying if the social context of our common life changes, our religious experience changes with it. Doctrines of salvation which have grown up in one social context will be modified in another, sooner or later, smoothly, awkwardly or with baffling dissension.

So, what happened to the concept of salvation as the "Cinderella" story became, over time, inaccessible to many? We say, abstractly, it became Arminian. I shall try to say what happened more imaginatively, more existentially.

In the more liberal churches that would one day be called Unitarian, the "Cinderella" story morphed. Call the new version the "Cynthia" story. Cynthia was born to parents who lived in "court circles," in the church. Maybe her father was a "court officer," an elder. Anyhow, Cynthia had known the Prince, to some extent, all her life, since childhood. As she neared adulthood, she learned from her minister's sermons that the king had said the Prince should think of marriage and that some thought of her as a good match for him.

Thus it came about that Cynthia and the Prince began a discreet courtship to see if they were, in fact, suited to one another. And thus Cynthia slowly became aware that, actually, she had loved the Prince, in a childish way, for as long as she could remember. As their courtship grew more serious, her love for him slowly deepened and became quite profound—all the more so as she and the Prince considered how important would be their shared responsibilities in future for the entire realm, the larger society. True, there were stages in their relationship, but they were stages of maturation, as from seedling to bud to flower. The day of this soul's spiritual "union" could not be dated; it had happened bit-by-bit. Nor was her membership in the church ever an issue. In the church her spiritual love had, not dramatically, but gradually, matured and grown, as had her keen sense of spiritual responsibility for the world at large.

It is impossible to say just when conservatives and liberals diverged in the Standing Order. In all the churches congregational polity was taken for granted. And both the "Cinderella" and "Cynthia" concepts of salvation were grounded in the spirit of mutual love. So these two concepts could—and did—coexist in the same churches for a long time. There came a time, though, when conservatives began to say to liberals, "You've changed the whole gospel story! You're preaching heresy!" Literally, conservatives criticized liberals for omitting the "peculiar" doctrines of the gospel. They meant the "peculiar" doctrines of God's utterly arbitrary selection of some people as his "Bride," the rest of humanity being doomed to everlasting punishment, of God's absolute omnipotence and omniscience, of predestination and human depravity, all of which are absent from the story of "Cynthia." Liberals had slowly and quietly rejected them (and not casually or carelessly, but with detailed and thorough study of the Bible and church history).

Many, many UUs have—ever since—thrown up their hands in frustration or fury over those "peculiar" doctrines, saying, "They're crazy and crazy-making!" I wholly agree. They are. We were and we are right to be rid of them. And yet, I think we need to be able to imagine why these doctrines had such convincing power for our early North American ancestors, that our alienation from our own heritage might diminish, that we might more clearly claim its treasures. So I ask you to think again of how much "falling in love" is celebrated in our present culture.

When we "fall" in love, helplessness is a part and parcel of the experience. "Falling in love" is not something we decide and choose to do of our own volition. That's part of its charm. Unless it turns out we've "fallen for" a creep, it's a wonderful experience we celebrate the more because it happened *to us*. And then we get on with the rest of our lives, never doubting that, for the most part, we are quite able to decide and choose. We hold this truth to be self-evident: Over the course of human events, we do not control all our experience all the time, but this does not imply that we should logically be either theological or philosophical determinists!

But historically, often in the West, when ecstatically "falling in love" with God has become the *central* concern of a religious leader or group, the helplessness of that experience has assumed theological significance. In our case, our Puritan forebears took the helplessness of their salvific experience to be a demonstration of philosophically necessary truths: that God's omnipotent power is manifest in human impotence to escape sin; that we must be born vile, utterly depraved; that the omniscient God must always have known and chosen whom he would save. These doctrines of God and humanity seemed to our Puritan forebears logically entailed in the experience of mutual love on which they based their—and our—doctrine of the church.

But were these awful doctrines ever really so entailed? I say they never were. Our New England founders were mistaken, not in the central importance of the spirit of mutual love in an authentic church, but in their inferences from the helplessness of ecstatic love. With a curious inconsistency, they didn't notice that when their attention turned from the ecstasy of salvation to issues of governance—in the church or in civil government—these "awful doctrines" often dropped out of mind. In Lecture 1, I pointed out their complete absence from the record of that year of Dedham conversations about the church, 1637. With the same curious inconsistency, the Cambridge Synod of 1648 voted to approve England's Winchester Confession "for the substance thereof ... [e]xcepting *only* some sections," and thus, "leaving the matter of discipline [that is, authority] to our own declaration thereof" [emphasis added]. Only! The Winchester Confession was consistent with the "awful doctrines." The Cambridge Platform, the New England churches' declaration of the doctrine of congregational—covenantal—polity, is not.

Arguments over this "curious inconsistency," over the theology of God and human nature, finally erupted early in the 1800s, in the Unitarian Controversy. When the dust had settled, the Standing Order was no more, and we Unitarians were a separate communion. How did our Unitarian churches do at cooperating with one another then?

Unitarian evangelism: who needs churches to build churches?

Life went on as it long had in most Unitarian churches. Many were large urban congregations of hundreds of families, with a Sunday worship attendance of six or eight hundred. (Theodore Parker's 28th Congregational drew between three and seven thousand, but that was an exception.) Many churches also had a rich program life during the week, of youth groups, groups meeting to do charity work, various study groups and so on.

But many Unitarians were deeply wounded from battles they had never wanted to fight. They had believed people of a loving Christian spirit could live together in the same churches, no matter what their differences. Then they had been accused of hypocrisy and deception for not making much of these differences. So, liberal leaders reluctantly set forth their case, with plain and careful arguments, laden with explanation of biblical references. Opponents were not persuaded. Soon, liberal ministers were excluded from pulpit exchanges in conservative churches.

Then within the walls of Harvard University—long the fount of Unitarian theology—Ralph Waldo Emerson delivered his "Divinity School Address" in 1838. He implied that Unitarian ministers in general preached without "soul." His "Address" set off the Transcendentalist flapdoodle. A bevy of bright young Transcendentalists—lay and ordained—made themselves as hard to get along with as possible, for a generation and more. Moreover, in this period there occurred the bitter conflict of the Hollis Street Church in Boston, over the minister's preaching against the Commonwealth's alcohol policies. The council summoned could be of no help. Of course, councils had not been able to help either during the Unitarian Controversy, which split many churches. But after the Hollis Street uproar no Unitarian church ever called a council again. That long-standing lateral pattern of cooperation among the churches vanished. And with it, the very notion that even strong and healthy churches need one another, not to mention weaker churches who get may stuck in a narrow, parochial view of what a liberal church is about.

A few—a very few—said Unitarians should organize themselves and make plans to grow as the country was growing. But most ministers resisted doing any such thing for 40 years. Why?

(1) They had no precedent for doing so. Since colonial days, new churches had gathered themselves, as settlers moved west a few miles. They had needed no special urging or assistance.

(2) The ministers looked back at how their own congregations had become Unitarian, gradually, quietly. Doubtless in future, they said, the same would happen in many now conservative churches.

(3) Just as, generations ago, the whole idea of the covenant had got tangled in a doctrine of history, now liberals took their own experience of stages of *maturation* to imply stages of *progress* in history, with the "signs" of progress clearly to be seen in America, actually, most clearly in New England. (This was at least as early as the 1820s, years before Darwin's books, and a large part of the reason Unitarians readily accepted Darwin's theory of evolution.) Some doctrine of history is always still another element—the 10th on our list—of any doctrine of the church. With a too-optimistic doctrine of history, the conditioned character of human destiny tends to drop out of mind. It leads to a loss of urgency in the members' sense of mission. Love itself comes to be taken as just natural, as needing no special communal focus or nurture. In our case the idea of progress seemed to justify doing nothing special, in the way of

organized cooperation, other than what the churches had been doing for 200 years. Progress in religion would come of itself, gradually, as from seedling to bud to flower.

(4) Most importantly, a new institutional pattern had reached New England and spread in the early 1800s with amazing speed—the *nonprofit corporation*. Today, we take this pattern so entirely for granted, we forget how young it is, historically.

Business corporations had been around a long time. But even in the 1700s, a few people couldn't just pool their capital, file some government forms, and start a new business. The king had a monopoly on monopolies. It was the king's prerogative to charter only such corporations as he chose. It took Adam Smith's *Wealth of Nations* and hard political struggle to win "the free market," the right of any group who can raise the needed capital to form a business corporation. But that right was finally enshrined in English law.

A business corporation—especially a large one, such as developed for the first time in England's Industrial Revolution—is usually a steep hierarchy, with owners of capital in control of a small governing board, which controls a small executive staff, which controls the mass of workers. So you might think Unitarians in New England, a deeply religious people, with a 200 year-old congregational tradition, would never relocate authority to the top of a governing structure like that of a business corporation, leaving people in the churches with little or none. But we have to take account of this cultural development in New England, in which the theology of covenantal organization never even came to mind.

It started with somebody's brainstorm in England. Why couldn't a few people form a corporation to do some some good and generous thing—like give away Bibles to poor people? They would not need their own capital, just people on a board of excellent reputation, whom others would trust, and the public would give the corporation money to distribute Bibles. Board members "of excellent reputation" would not have time to do this work, but they could use donated funds to hire an executive staff to see to the work. With that brilliant idea the British Bible Society was born. It was a huge success. Money poured in; Bibles poured out. The more Bibles it gave away, the more money people gave to this nonprofit corporation.

What a switch! Religious people, no doubt, but not the churches *per se*, adopting the hierarchical structure of a business corporation, to spend money from donors for charitable purposes, over which the donors had not a smidgen of control. In the bat of an eye, historically speaking, all kinds of reform movements were afoot in New England, urged on and organized by nonprofit corporations, to address immigrant poverty, to educate orphans, to advocate freedom for the slaves, to institute tax support for public schools, for peace, against alcohol, for woman's suffrage, and on and on. (Conrad Edick Wright tells the story of this institutional revolution in his 1992 book *The Transformation of Charity in Postrevolutionary New England*.) Unitarians were leading figures in all these efforts and held board positions in many, many of these nonprofit corporations.

Thus it came to be that, over time and with a curious inconsistency, when Unitarians turned their attention from governance of the local church to any good work beyond the walls of the local church, we took for granted the hierarchical structure of a nonprofit corporation, even for gathering new Unitarian churches!

In 1825 a few Unitarians adopted this new model and organized a Unitarian nonprofit. They sought no vote of approval from members of the congregations. The congregations had nothing to do with it. A few people simply started another nonprofit corporation and called it the American Unitarian Association. Made up of a board, a small, part-time staff and, spasmodically, a few volunteers, it was a missionary enterprise, its purpose to raise money for starting new churches, or at least "to diffuse pure Christianity" by distributing pamphlets and books.

The AUA was not well supported. For the next 40 years, it had an average income of about $8,000 a year. Even so, the AUA slowly acquired informal authority, an authority never delegated to it by local churches. In 1865—40 years later—a Conference of Unitarian churches was at last organized, with great enthusiasm and much lay participation. The Conference in one year raised $100,000 and turned it over to the "traditional" executive board of the AUA, even though the AUA still had no institutional ties with the churches at all.

Well, it's been a while since 1825. Our institutional path to the 21st century has been twisty and wind-y. Maybe all such paths are. In these lectures I shall not tell the tale of how the AUA of 1825 became the UUA of 2001, which has essentially the same corporate board/staff structure of 1825. "Delegates" from our churches now elect the UUA board and its president—our "chief executive officer"—even though the pyramidal shape of a board/staff structure is, by definition, topsy-turvy from that of congregational—or covenantal—polity, and even though none of our leaders have ever been able to elicit much glad cooperation from us within such a hierarchal structure. The fact is we never have—to this day—thought much about our patterns of cooperation among churches or the structure of our Association as elements of our liberal doctrine of the church.

I saw a sentence on a website recently, which illustrates how unaware many UUs are of how and why we ever started doing things as we do. The sentence read, " Unitarians were not organized as a sect until the founding of the AUA in 1825." That tiny group in the AUA, a sect! In an era when Unitarian churches were unanimously agreed that our churches should be non-sectarian!

Here, in two sentences, is the thesis of these lectures. *Our UU churches are uncooperative, not because congregational polity is our doctrine of the church. Rather, our churches are uncooperative—and far too many are weak and ineffective—because our organization needs to be more covenantal, both in our congregations and among the congregations of our Association.*

To worship and serve and grow and thrive, as we have it in us to do, we need now to invent new covenantal structures for more free cooperation among us than we have had since our earliest days on this continent. We've come a long way in many ways since the founding of our oldest churches in the 1630s. The spirit of mutual love is yet that reality most worthy of our ultimate loyalty, our religious loyalty. Our love, though seldom of the ecstatic variety, is warm and steady and deep and powerful to redeem and to enhance our own lives and many more lives in our larger world. We might yet enter a covenant to walk together in this spirit as an association of free congregations, without hierarchy, but with many well-used lateral patterns of engagement, in which we respect each congregation's independence and our interdependence in the interdependent web of existence of which it is our blessed privilege to be a part. I pray we may yet do so.

Lecture 4: The Theology and Anthropology of Our Liberal Covenant

Love is the doctrine of this church . . .
Thus do we covenant with each other and with God.

These familiar lines are the theme of this year's six Minns Lectures. I thank you for coming to hear this afternoon's Lecture 4 on the theology and anthropology of our liberal covenant. Our understanding of the way things are, and should be and could be with us human beings: that is our anthropology. Our understanding of what is holy, most precious, most salutary, most worthy of our devotion and faithfulness: that is our theology. The two subjects are inseparable. Each always reflects and implies the other. Everybody is a theologian and an anthropologist—to the extent that all of us have to try to make some sense of ourselves and the world, as a condition of sanity. I have been trying, in this Minns Lecture series, to get us to see our liberal doctrine of the church as having been shaped by events of our history, for which we need a critical appreciation in order to understand who we are as a religious people. I will continue that effort later in this presentation. But I want to come at the topics of the day by talking about language.

An amazing thing happens when we human beings communicate, using words, on the most ordinary of occasions. Certainly, miscommunication is frequent, among any people. But that fact is easier to explain than that we ever communicate—or transfer meaning—at all, which we do, with astonishing precision, every day! We do so, even though the meanings of our words change, all the time, and at greatly varying rates.

Often, old words come to carry new meanings, right along with ancient meanings, without confusion and very quickly. For example, think of the new meanings and the much older meanings now carried by these words: enter, touch, send, return, save, scroll, click, icon, mouse, bite, memory, dot, window, web. Somehow, we are able easily to distinguish the new meanings from the old, according to the context of usage.

Not long ago, recently, a few computer geeks assigned new meanings to all these old words. And, a few years later, tens of millions of us have so integrated these new meanings that we can use them metaphorically. You could dash off a note, to a friend you haven't seen in years, and tack onto the end this sentence, "When I think of you, I click on save."

Just 10 or 15 years ago your friend might well have received that sentence as gibberish. But now he or she would not write back to ask, "What do you mean—you 'click on save' when you think of me?"

If he or she did ask, an explanation would go something like this: "I love you, faraway Friend, and I will love you in future, so much do I treasure memories of you from our past. But these days, if I said so straight out, I would sound too mushy, goopy. So, I will use the working of a computer as a metaphor, for my mind and heart. Computers, of course, are high speed, electronic machines, without mind or heart, so far as we know. But the way a human mind works is somewhat like the way a computer works. And, for metaphorical purposes, we can bracket—or set aside—the computer's unlikeness to a human being. I focus on a certain likeness, and I represent a human being as working like a computer. I say, 'When I think of you, I click on save.' And you will correctly interpret my words as pointing to two realities: (1) my abiding affection for you, and (2) our shared understanding that a light-hearted tone is right for our time. Of course, neither affection nor the right tone of a message is at all like a computer. Still, you get my point: I am glad that you—though a long way off—are part of who I am."

We use metaphors in our speech many, many times every day. Their effectiveness comes of our human ability to compare things, to see how they are alike and—for the purposes of communication—to suppress their unlikeness and focus on a certain likeness. Thus we communicate meaning in one area of our lives, with reference to another.

Isn't this marvelous? A 10-year-old who never heard of metaphors and has never once thought about how they work, a child in our time could send—to a buddy his own age or to his grandmama—a note saying, "When I think of you, I click on save." Yet only if the new meanings, of a whole cluster of words, can be distinguished from old meanings in a nanosecond by tens of millions of others in the same culture, according to the context of usage.

In a real sense, then, even a private note, sent and received, is not just a private transfer of meaning between two people. Rather, it is one communication made possible by these two individuals' participation in each other's lives and by their participation in a third reality, a vast and dynamic network of meaning, in which all of us, who live in the same world and speak the same language, live and move and have our being. Though we may seldom—or never—think of this vast and dynamic network of meaning, we are utterly dependent on it, all the time, for the expression or understanding of any meaning at all. We can distinguish a private note within this third reality, so far exceeding ourselves. We cannot separate a private note from its much larger context. The private note could not be except that it is part of the other. The private note is not a separate or separable thing of itself.

I ask you to focus on this third reality, this network of meanings. There are prevailing patterns in it. These patterns are interactive with us; that is, with our usage the patterns are modified over time. But, though they change, there are, always, patterns. With reference to language, we call these the rules of grammar. We try to teach these rules to children in school. But the fact is, toddlers learn them without instruction. Two-year-old Susie says, "I want a cookie," not, "Cookie a want I." Even toddlers know that to communicate using words, we must act in accord with prevailing patterns of the network, its rules. We cannot arbitrarily scramble our words. You could not meaningfully write to your friend, "Save click think you, on when I of I." Our freedom of speech is conditioned. Our freedom stands under judgment. To communicate creatively and freely, we must act in accord with patterns of meaning we did not make, or else ruin the possibility of free speech.

Right there we have an illustration of the great paradox of covenantal anthropology and theology: *Authentic human freedom is by necessity lawful freedom.* Moreover, the patterns or laws or rules of the network are not rightly understood if they are seen as there to restrain or inhibit or control us, although we will be barred from participating in meaning if we disregard them. Rather, these patterns make meaning possible. We rightly see ourselves as wonderfully gifted with discernment, gifted in that we can perceive these patterns and learn more of them and be still more creatively free within them.

I hope you see that I am now pointing to an analogy, a likeness: The patterns of meaning which make language possible are analogous to other natural laws. Though the universe within which we dwell is dynamic, not static, it is lawful. That is, there are consequences of obeying and of breaking natural laws; the universe is responsive to human beings, in that at least some of the patterns vital to us as human beings change over time, in response to our usage, but there are, always, patterns we cannot flout without loss of meaningful life. That is a theological statement.

I am also lifting up certain features of an anthropology, a notion of what it means to be human. Namely, as a race or species of creatures, we are both *limited,* or governed, by an authority greater than our own, and *free.* We are supported by and gifted by the way things are, and we are obliged to be responsible for what we do with our gifts in our freedom. We can be appreciative and obedient, creative and constructive, and if we are, these actions will have consequences. And we can be willfully or mistakenly disobedient and destructive and mess up our own freedom; if we do, these actions will have consequences.

Because, then, authentic human freedom is, of necessity, lawful freedom, and because we receive the possibility of freedom as a gift of the way things are, an authentic covenant is: a glad promise to live freely together, insofar as we are able, in accordance with the laws of reality that make our freedom possible. This is true whether the agreement is between just two, as in a union of marriage, or whether the agreement is among millions, as in a free nation, or whether the agreement is among members who gather to be a free congregation. Any authentic covenant will be based on a mutually shared understanding of the patterns or laws of a third reality. The third reality of a covenant is, not just of the network of a language, but the whole of being. Using a metaphor taken from the realm of ecology, we UUs have recently taken to calling this third reality "the interdependent web of existence of which we are a part." God is a shorter name for that reality greater than all, yet present in each.

A little more about language. "When I think of you, I click on save." I have spoken of three realities of this one little sentence: (1) abiding affection, (2) a light-hearted tone and (3) a vast web of meaning, patterned yet also ever changing, a dynamic network of meanings. I trust no one would say, "But those are not realities." Because, of course, they are. They are self-evident realities of our experience, part of our everyday lives, though they are measureless realities. We cannot locate the edges, the limits, of these things. That is, we cannot define them, as we can a house or a tree or a mountain or a computer. We can only speak of a measureless reality by comparing it with some limited, measurable reality. That is what we do when we use metaphors.

One example: Consider the word base. We speak of the base of a house or a tree or a mountain. We speak of the basic binary mathematics of a computer. We are talking about measurable things. But suppose your sister is puzzled by a friend of yours and by the fact that you have begun going, often, to her church. And so she says to you, "What is the basis of your affection for this person? I find her basically calculating, cold as a computer. And that religion of hers—what is it based on?"

I trust you hear the metaphor in these questions. Does affection or a religion rest its weight on a base, as a house or a tree or a mountain does? No. Affection and religion don't have weight, except metaphorically, in comparison with some measurable thing. Nor is human temperament a function of a mathematical design, except metaphorically, in comparison with a machine. Yet a metaphor is effective so long as we focus on the likeness of measurable and measureless realities and bracket—set aside—their *unlikeness*. On the other hand, though a metaphor may have worked well for many, many people for a very long time, it will break down and be useless to us once we focus on the unlikeness of things we are comparing.

Let's look at one example of a broken religious metaphor. Recently, some UU ministers were having a conversation. One got to talking, whose UU church is in a predominantly Lutheran part of the country. As you may know, most Lutherans address their minister as Pastor Luopa, or Pastor Morgan, or just Pastor. This UU minister was saying how awkward she feels when folks out in the larger community—even people who aren't Lutheran, Catholics—address her as Pastor Jones. She doesn't want to correct them. That would seem nit-picky and make them feel awkward. Still, she feels funny—phony—letting people call her that when our UU members never would.

Other ministers tried to ease her discomfort. They said things like, "But we talk about the pastoral side of ministry. All our students for the ministry have to do CPE, Clinical Pastoral Education. When we have to be away, we ask a colleague to be on call for emergency pastoral care and so on. So, don't worry about it."

But another minister said, "I hate the word pastor. *Pastor* is Latin for shepherd. People in UU churches are not sheep. I never let anybody call me that."

I thought, Oh, dear! Why is this good man so prickly about a word? I'm pretty sure Lutherans don't think of people in their churches as sheep. But in their anthropology, Lutherans have historically focused attention on the common need, of all human beings and other creatures, for loving care. When Lutherans call their ministers Pastor, that's the likeness to many living things they're focused on. Lutheran pastors are leaders of groups of people for whom loving and caring are very important. We in our tradition have historically focused more on the need of human beings for independent thinking. When humans can't think with a measure of independence, we act like sheep and can be herded about. It's not that we want our ministers to be unloving or uncaring! But in our anthropology, we focus on the unlikeness of people and sheep, herd animals. So the metaphor of the minister as shepherd, or God as shepherd, has broken down for us. We can't use that metaphor, or if we do, we're restive with it. It doesn't feel right. The tone is wrong.

Well, my attention had wandered. I was not—sheeplike—following the conversation, but thinking my own independent thoughts. But a bit later the same minister, who had declared so strongly that UUs are not sheep, was again speaking. He was recommending, for reading in a worship service, a favorite poem of his titled, "Be Like a Duck."

I thought, Gee! This colleague thinks it's bad to be like a sheep, but good to be like a duck. I'd better listen. He read us the poem. It was about a duck gliding along on a placid lake on a beautiful day. I would say the message of the poem was something like this: We can trust the interdependent web of existence of which we are a part, even though, sometimes, all about us is trouble and confusion. At the core of our being, we can be, religiously, in spirit, not fearful and distressed, but like a duck gliding along on a placid lake on a beautiful day.

Hmm, I thought. The message of that poem is very like another. "The Lord is my shepherd. . . . He leadeth me beside the still waters. . . . Yea, though I walk through the valley of the shadow of death, . . . thy rod and thy staff, they comfort me."

The aim of valid religious, metaphorical language—though it be of shepherds and sheep or lakes and ducks—is to communicate the meaning of measureless realities which, though they be measureless, are very important, everyday realities of our lives.

Traditional covenant language: to what everyday realities did it point?

The word "covenant" has come to us by means of the Bible. The covenant is a metaphor taken first in our cultural history, not from the phenomena of language, but from the realm of politics. In the very ancient Near East, politics seldom rose above the level of a protection racket. Various warlords, or just gang leaders, having acquired a following of tough guys and some weapons, made their living by raiding defenseless farmers and herders, stealing their crops and animals. In an agricultural economy such raids, especially repeated raids, meant a very hard life indeed for many people.

Eventually, a warlord might come along, strong enough to call himself a king. This king and his army would round up the smaller gangs and do them in, or bring them into his army and discipline them. No more freelance raiding. Then the king would call together all the heads of families and clans of the region he had pacified, and say something like this:

"My name is Great So-and-So, king of your world. With my great power I have put down your enemies. Thanks to me, you may now live and prosper in peace, on certain conditions. You will send me an annual tribute. Whenever I require your service in my army, you will send at once the number of men I call for. And you will sign a covenant, promising to keep faith with me, your king. Moreover, just so nobody forgets, you will store this writing in a sacred place, and you will come together like this, annually, and read it aloud to the whole population, so that everybody will know: You are my people; I am your king. You keep your word; I'll keep mine, and things will go well with you. Break your covenant with me, and I promise I will make you very, very sorry."

That way of keeping down raiding gang leaders and warlords became the traditional way kings established their realms and kept order throughout the region. A scholar, George Mendenhall, in the 20th century CE, found such covenants all over the ancient Near East. Sometimes, perhaps, this was a good enough arrangement, if the king and his generals did not get too greedy. But, as the history of the world amply demonstrates to this present day, where peace and prosperity, for the vast majority of the people, depend on the moderate desires of human kings and generals for wealth and power, the people can depend on nothing but oppression and misery. When those on top get greedy and build for themselves splendid palaces—while the people live in hovels—and get addicted to ever more power than they need to keep order, the shape of a monstrous pyramid is the shape of the entire social structure. It weighs very heavily on, crushes, the freedom of the masses at the bottom.

At some point in time—at what point is for anthropologists and historians to argue—some genius, somebody who had seen much of how kings and generals generally operate, came up with a new metaphor taken from the protection-racket model of politics. This metaphor is based on an unlikeness: The King of the Universe is not like these human kings.

"The Ruler of the realm of all nature is generous, not greedy. He makes the grass and the fruits of the earth to grow, the rains to fall and the sun to shine for all the creatures of the earth. Thus he shows his love for all the world. How can we not love God in return! Moreover, our Creator causes us human beings to love one another and our land and animals, as

72

he loves us. We do not need these human kings. We can enter into a political and religious covenant with each other and with God the King of the Universe to be ruled by his holy ways of love and generosity.

"We must draw everyone into this covenant, even the least and the weakest, even the gang leaders who sometimes rise up among us. For if we have not lived by the ways of love, our Creator has made us so that we can change our ways, start over and live by his laws. Our freedom to change is a gift of his forgiveness and mercy. If we freely cooperate, because we love, we can protect ourselves against would-be kings and other invaders. We can assemble to fight at the sound of the shofar. But when we have done what we have to do to protect ourselves, we will return to our homes and lay down our weapons. Let the nations around us fight and rage. We will not. We will live every one under his vine and fig tree and keep covenant with one another and with our God, King of the Universe. *All he requires of us—blessed be he—is that we love him and love our neighbors as ourselves, and keep the natural, common-sense laws of a peaceful community because we love.*"

Who was the genius who invented this covenantal metaphor? Assigned new meaning to the old words, king and covenant? Was it Noah? Or Abraham? Or Moses? It doesn't matter. What matters is that the idea of a freely-entered covenant—with the very nature of loving and lawful reality—became the root idea of the political religion of a people, the ancient Israelites. The Israelites told each other and wrote down stories about their political and religious covenant and their attempts—and their failures—to keep covenant with each other and with God. They created a literature which nourished their memories and their hopes. They fed their dedication to a loving and freely cooperative way of life with stories of their great King of the Universe and his care for them, as well as the wrath of his anger when they broke their covenant with him, by doing wrong to one another. Our modern understanding of political democracy evolved from our ancestors' engagement with and adaptations of Israelite stories. American democracy was born when members of our own oldest churches in New England focused their attention on the oldest stories in the Bible and said, "We don't need a human king either. We, too, can be free to live in covenantal fealty, in faithful love, to each other and to God."

73

The most ancient Israelites were a rural people and, probably in the earliest days, a polyglot people of many races. For their small country was at the crossroads of great surrounding empires. They did not themselves long do without a human king, maybe a few centuries. Then they had the same kind of problems too much power in the hands of too few always brings. Yet again and again, there also rose up preachers—prophets, in Hebrew *nabi*—to speak hard truth to power. The prophets said, over and over again, "The ways of greed and coercion are in violation of God's patterns. These ways will not work. If you think they will, you are deceived. They will suck you and the land with you into ruin. Turn to the ways of love and justice for the oppressed. For these ways are the ways of the King of the Universe, whose laws are loving and just because he is loving and just, and he demands that we be like him in all our ways."

Ancient Israel broke into two kingdoms, northern Israel and southern Judah, when its third king, Solomon's son, tried to assume the throne. Eventually, the northern kingdom was defeated and the people exiled by a neighboring empire in the eighth century BCE. Judah was also defeated and the people exiled to Babylon in the sixth century BCE. When Babylonia was defeated, the Persian king Cyrus allowed the exiles to go home. Cyrus is spoken of in our English translation of the Old Testament as God's anointed one. The Greek word for anointed one is *christos*, the Hebrew *messiah*.

But ancient Israel was never again a self-governing country, except for one brief period, before the Romans took over. Israel was ruled by the satraps of great empires. Yet this most political of religions lived on into Roman times, even when there were more Jews in the great cities of Egypt, Persia, Greece and Rome than there were in Palestine. In Roman times, another prophet began to preach and teach, Jesus of Nazareth. The books of the New Testament tell of his life and the lives of some of those who learned from him, his disciples. Testament is a synonym for covenant. The New Testament tells stories of Mediterranean people, ruled by Rome, *who entered a new covenant, not as a nation, but as individuals of many nations, in the covenant of free congregations.*

What was new about this new covenant? The meanings of words change, all the time, at varying rates, as old metaphors are broken and new ones are invented. So I shall try to say what was new about the covenant of the earliest Christian churches, using other words than those we associate with orthodox Judaism or Christianity. Freedom to use new words to transfer old meaning is part of the authentic and lawful freedom of a liberal.

Jesus thought like a sociologist and a linguist. That is to say, he understood that the metaphor of the covenant with the King of the Universe had become hopelessly confused with the language of coercive governments. His people were now thinking of the King of the Universe as more *like* than *unlike* human kings.

So, Jesus basically said, "Look, you are obsessed with Caesar and his power. Bracket Caesar. Set Caesar aside. Sure the government controls much of your life, far too much. But no human ruler, not even the Roman Emperor, can control all life. You want to know what is holy? What we can count on? What we ought to be most faithful to? How we ought to shape our own lives, insofar as we can? Look at the flowers of the field and the birds of the air. Look at how seeds sprout and grow. Focus on these things. Appreciate and be grateful for the generous ways of God the Father (rather than the King of the Universe).

"Above all look at ordinary, everyday human love, of parents for their children and children for their parents. And look inside your own heart at your ability to change, to go from treating others as crassly and meanly as Caesar treats you, to the more normal, healthy ways of a loving spirit."

And Jesus and his disciples spoke politically; that is, with regard for organization. They said, "Lord knows, it is not always easy to figure out what are the ways of love! But even in this empire, we can form covenanted congregations we decide to enter, one by one, and help each other live in a context far larger than the puny Roman Empire which—however strong it looks—will fade sooner or later, as all empires do. Caesar will not like our forming congregations and meeting to worship and to help one another discern what love requires of us. He will hound us and persecute us for presuming to claim our ultimate loyalty is to something bigger and more important than he is. But, unless we let him intimidate us, he cannot stop anything like all of us from organizing to worship and to learn to live freely in accord with the laws of love."

What would Jesus' message sound like if addressed to our time? I think, something like this: "Look, I know some of you think all the power that matters is in the human hands of Wall Street traders, the grossly deceiving advertising industry and the grossly shallow entertainment industry of America. Well, if you are obsessed with that piece of the world, if all you do, basically, is go to work, watch television and seek out other entertainment, you might think that piece of the world is the whole world. It is not. There is a great deal more to life than working for huge corporations, finding some ever-new distraction or buying ever more things. Be gathered into communities of love. Find, together, what is more meaningful, more loving, more worthy of your attention, and be empowered in devotion to these things. Seek and ye shall find. Knock and it shall be opened to you. The truth will make you free."

Our contemporary liberal covenant

I begin this section by giving utterance to some questions. I put it to you that there is one correct answer to every one of them. The correct answer is not an explanation of anything but, rather, a fit, an appropriate exclamation. The correct answer to all these questions is: God! I don't know!

How big is the universe in which we are this moment alive?

How long will it last?

Why—not how, but why—is there such an event as human life?

Every person we know is more than we will ever know; we never even know all of ourselves. How is it we so often forget that we dwell all our lives in mystery?

Why do human beings need so urgently to love and be loved?

Is love just a human requirement, or is it a feature of the whole universe?

Why is it, even when we human beings have all our bodily needs met, we can become so alienated that we hate our own lives, and are only terribly bored or angry or lonely or frightened, though the world holds much that we could not help loving, if we but noticed and paid attention, let these things speak to us?

76

Why is it we human beings can come to love things and devote all our energies to gaining access to things patently bad for us, even poison, like drugs or alcohol, or to acquiring far more money than we need, or far more power over others than anybody needs, or status, or fame—when none of these things turn out to be worth what we have to do to get them?

How many events are going on right now which will greatly affect us in future, of which we presently know nothing?

Why is it that we are gifted with such imagination that we can learn of and understand and love realms of reality and other cultures in which we have never set foot, and yet we may also be led by our imagination into delusion and craziness?

How is it that we can sometimes see patterns in the way the world works, and sometimes not? How many times do we wrestle and wrestle with some problem, work and work with the data, and then suddenly, just see meaning we didn't see earlier? We say, "Why didn't I think of this before?"

Or, we hear somebody else's good idea and we say, "Of course. Why didn't I think of that?"

Or, we are reminded of something very important, which we already knew, and we say, "How on earth could I have forgotten this?"

Language itself can serve as a metaphor. It is metaphorically correct to say reality addresses human beings, speaks to us, and summons our love, our understanding and our humility—when we are open, passive, receptive to what it has to say. Thus the compound meanings of the word *logos* in Greek. The *logos* is the *word* reality has spoken to us; the *logos* is *natural law*; the *logos* is *reason* or *logic* greater than all, yet present in each.

The questions I read are not questions we human beings just make up on our own. Rather, to be human is to be engaged in a ceaseless dialogue, a conversation, not only with each other but with the nature of reality. Reality addresses us, and we respond with questions. Or, as Martin Buber once said, we may have it backwards when we suppose we pose these unanswerable questions. It may be that God always poses the ultimate question, as in the Book of Job. "Where were you when I created the world?" The only correct answer is, "God! I don't know!" And strangely, the rational humility of that answer is not humiliating, but salutary, healing and empowering. When Job is rightly humbled of heart, he can get up from the ashes of despair and get on with a blessed life, taking advantage—whatever has gone before—of the new possibilities reality constantly presents to us.

It makes sense to me to believe all the great religious traditions of the world began with somebody's extraordinary insight into what, in all this great buzzing banging, blooming and silent mystery, *really matters most for human beings to love, to understand, to trust and be faithful to, because it is life-giving and life-enhancing.* If anybody wants to call such extraordinary insight revelation, it's all right by me. The question of revelation is: Why should one person or one group ever understand anything and others not? God! I don't know why. But what is truly wonderful about extraordinary insights is this: They can be communicated, shared, taught to others who then see them too, and then whole cultures are generated from them. Our word religion derives from the same root present in the word ligament. Without healthy and importantly true religious insights into the mystery of our lives, we're like Ezekiel's pile of dry and unconnected bones, with no ligaments. A vital religion keeps us tied together, so we can stand up and move and get things done and live, with love and meaning, together, when a healthy cult is the heart of a culture.

All religions must use metaphors to express insights into the nature of reality, metaphors taken from our everyday experience, because there's no other way to express them. Some metaphors may serve very well and last a long time. But all of them are ultimately fragile and subject to erosion and distortion. Hence, the need for reform of the language of every religion, over and over and over.

You and I stand, as Unitarian Universalists, in the long tradition of the covenantal free church. We add the adjective liberal and say ours is a liberal free church, meaning—our everyday world has forced upon us the recognition that no one religious tradition has a monopoly on right love and truth. We infer, from our encounters with other traditions, that there have been and are people of extraordinary insight into what really matters for human beings, in every time and clime. Therefore, though the depths of our own tradition are more available to us—through inheritance—and are the depths from which we must live, we want to and we will try to be open to others. We are not exclusivists, claiming our way is the only good way. Yet, we do specially treasure our own religious tradition precisely for its *political relevance*, for its constant reminder to us that *human freedom and human health is a function of how we organize socially*, what is the shape of our economic and governmental—and religious—institutions.

You and I stand, as Unitarian Universalists, in the long tradition of the covenantal free church. We add the adjective humanist and say ours is a humanist tradition—meaning our everyday world has forced upon us the recognition that *valid religious insights, even the most extraordinary, are always rooted in ordinary human experience of concrete events.* To know anything at all about reality in general—or God—we make inferences from our limited experience to great encompassing truths, not the other way around. Therefore, even those insights we claim and stake our lives on are to be stated humbly, not in a doctrinaire fashion, always with the awareness that we might be wrong. *Faith* is best understood, not as certainty, but *as sufficient confidence and trust in what we have been given and called to do that we can be faithful, together, covenantally.* We can—thank God!—be faithful to what we cannot help believing is true about the way things are with us, and should be and could be, because it makes sense to us. And when we break faith and break our covenant we can—thank God!—many and many a time accept the opportunity to begin again, begin anew to live faithfully, starting now. For this we cannot help believing: While the interdependent web of existence of which we are a part judges us and frustrates us, not only as individuals but as peoples, when we disregard or violate its laws, it is also gracious, offering us, over and over, new chances for the practice of authentic, creative, lawful and loving, redemptive freedom.

I will try in a few words to state, as simply and straightforwardly as I can, the anthropology and theology of a covenantal, liberal and humanist free church in our time. Can I do so in such a way as to win universal approval among us? Of course not. Even so, I trust that our—my and your—efforts to communicate our understanding of the most important realities of our lives are almost always beneficial—or as our ancestors would have said—good for our mutual edification.

We human beings are promising creatures, in more than one sense. We are born with promise, or potential, which we do not and cannot create—with the promise of intelligence, of appreciation, of creativity, of cooperation and, most importantly, of love. Our very capacities and capabilities are a gift to us of the way things are. Therefore, it is appropriate to begin our worship services with songs and prayers of praise and gratitude for all gifts, not made by human hands but by God. Even so, we are and ought to be pretty sparing in our use of the word God. It's a word easily abused, and most authentically used as an *exclamation*, in face of the wonder and splendor and mercy of our lives, even in the hardest of times.

We human beings are promising creatures, too, in the sense that we can only do great and worthy things—indeed we can only survive—when we make and keep promises of loyalty and faithfulness to the ways of love with others. For distinct and different as we are as individuals, we are also thoroughly social creatures. The options and choices we have as individuals are effected and affected by those of others; our decisions and actions and inaction effect and affect many others. None of us can fulfill our promise as individuals without the faithfulness and loyalty of many others. Therefore, the aim of our worship services is a renewal of our sense of gratitude for and loyalty to the spirit of love which summons and creates and re-creates *right* loyalties within us.

What is spirit? There's no saying precisely, because the reality we are talking about is measureless. Best point to our everyday uses of the word and leave it to each to make their own analogy. We talk of a spirit of generosity or a spirit of cooperation. We talk about the *esprit de corps* in a vital army unit or workforce. We talk about a healthy school spirit. We talk about spirited horses. When a friend is ill, we ask the family, "How are his spirits?" We do know what we mean by the phrase "spirit of mutual love," and that a free church exists wherever we enter into a covenant to live in this spirit, together, gathering regularly for public worship and for seeking truth together, for listening to and responding to each other, that we might teach and be taught. The mutual spirit of love is alone worthy of our greatest, our ultimate loyalty. For when we kill it, life loses its savor and we open ourselves to destructive, deadly evil, unworthy doing.

We human beings are also promise-breaking creatures. We violate our covenants in petty, small ways and in tragic, disastrous ways. Whether we do so out of sheer forgetfulness or poorly ordered priorities or ignorance or for motives we ourselves cannot admire, ill consequences are real for the whole interdependent web. Therefore, our worship services need to include time for reflection on our failures and mistakes, that we might be people of tender conscience, easily provoked to turn again toward the ways of love and do better tomorrow than we have done today. Love is a response to the loveliness, the charm, the good, the worth of an other. To be lifelong, passionately religious lovers is to learn and practice the precious disciplines of paying attention and being still, receptive to the lure of that beyond ourselves which awakens love in us. For when we rightly love, we rightly spend ourselves for the sake of the beloved and for the just character of our whole society.

We human beings, especially in a culture so complex as ours, are part of many communities. We need one—our freely covenanted church community—in which our purpose is to be reminded of and to take account of the promising character of human beings in the widest possible sense, that we may answer the summons, the call of all that is holy to live with authenticity and integrity and joy and resolve. For responsibility is a response to the way the world presents itself to us when we are paying attention and trying to discern the word it speaks to us, as mediated by and tested for sense in earnest and intentional, social dialogue.

It is certainly possible for people to be in an implicit covenant without saying so. They just gather and act together, freely, in love and for good ends. Recognition of this fact is at the heart of our concept of the church universal, that measureless company of people whose goodness has been and is effective in shaping human history throughout history. Yet it is also very important to distinguish between the church universal and a particular, concrete and local free church, lest our understanding of the free church become an empty abstraction, a fuzzy ideal bearing no relation to the everyday lives of actual people. Our local church covenant needs to be as clear and explicit as we can make it, that we may teach it to our children, as the reasonable explanation they deserve of why we do things as we do in this church, and that we may invite others—as many

81

others as will—to join us in making and renewing, again and again, our promise of loyalty to the ways of love that matter most in human life, that we might fulfill our promise. For the free church covenant is at bottom the covenant a free society requires. The creative freedom of our whole society will endure for just the length of time we together understand and teach and keep our covenant and speak with our own mouths the words of love and truth and freedom the whole world always needs to hear.

An appendix to Lecture 4:
One version of our liberal covenant

Though our knowledge is incomplete,
our truth partial and our love uneven,
From our own experience and from
the witness of our faith tradition
We believe
     that new light is ever waiting to break
     through individual hearts and minds
     to illumine the ways of humankind,
     that there is mutual strength
     in willing cooperation,
     and that the bonds of love keep open
     the gates of freedom.
Therefore we pledge
to walk together in the ways
 of truth and affection
as best we know them now
or may learn them in days to come
That we and our children may be fulfilled
And that we may speak to the world
with words and actions
of peace and goodwill.

Lecture 5:
Updating the Cambridge Platform

You have come to hear Lecture 5 of the 2000–01 Minns Lectures series of six. I've already said a lot in the earlier four lectures that has a bearing on how I finish. So, you might feel as we do when the only time we can get in to see a movie we want to see, is in the middle of a showing. It's hard to figure what the movie is about, when we haven't seen how it started.

So, I'll begin this evening by saying, Welcome to the world! For is this not part of what it means to be human? We are always born in the *middle* of stories. The dramas—of our families, our economy, our schools, our government—of our churches—began a long time ago. The patterns of people's ideas and assumptions, especially about authority and division of labor, and the plot line, the direction in which things are moving, or not going anywhere—all these patterns were set long before we even start to understand what is going on.

We Unitarian Universalists are part of a very long story of many, many people who—in the middle of the complex situations they were born into—at some point fervently declared, "The things in this story are not as they should be. There is a better way! And some of us are, by God, going to covenant to find and live out simpler, saner, more natural, holier ways of love."

We UUs derive from a long, tangled line of religious reformers. Maybe tangled is not the right word. But for sure the plot lines of our story—of how our Unitarian Universalist churches came to be as they are now—are complex.

We UUs are a liberal people over on the "left" of the free-church tradition. The root idea of our entire tradition is the covenant. A covenanted free church is a body of individuals who have freely made a profoundly simple promise, a covenant: *We pledge to walk together in the spirit of mutual love. The spirit of love is alone worthy of our ultimate, our religious loyalty. So, we shall meet often to take counsel concerning the ways of love, and we will yield religious authority solely to our own understanding of what these ways are, as best we can figure them out or learn or remember them, together.* But the story of how this simple idea has been, over and over, corrupted, or tangled up in authoritarianism, or forgotten and lost from actual lives and institutions and societies—this story is not simple at all.

The thesis of these lectures: (1) We UUs are the people we are in large part because we inherited the covenantal free-church tradition from the 17th-century founders of our oldest New England churches, who themselves reclaimed the tradition, when it had been nearly lost, from centuries before their time. (2) For much of the 19th and 20th centuries we UUs almost forgot the covenant. So, we need now a new critical appreciation of the best gifts and worst mistakes of our own covenantal history. And (3) we need now to do two things: to reclaim and creatively adopt covenants in our free churches, in our own liberal way, for our time, and to invent what we have never yet had, a Covenanted Association of Congregations. We need to do these things because too many of our churches are not thriving, and thriving, liberal free churches are the best hope of the world!

This evening I want us to look at the gifts and the mistakes we inherited from the 17th-century founders of our oldest UU churches, as these are manifest, with hindsight, in a document called the Cambridge Platform. I want first, though, to tell you a more personal story.

An example of institutional inventiveness

In the summer of 1973 Joe and our daughters and I moved to the Texas Gulf Coast. An experienced lay UU at age 36, I had just begun studying for our ministry. In 1973 the Southwest Conference had not had—in living memory—any women students for the ministry. And suddenly, you had three, two working in Dallas, and me in Chicago and Beaumont.

The Southwest ministers received us as graciously as they could, that is, with comical awkwardness. And the Southwest laypeople were wonderfully open and generous. In five years, from 1973 to 1978, I preached in 14 Southwest pulpits; I was secretary of the Conference board for a year; one summer I was the "sunset" preacher at the Summer Institute, SWUUSI; I interned at Houston's Emerson Church; and I served two congregations as minister, in College Station and Corpus Christi, for 18 and 9 months.

I wouldn't trade anything for what I learned here, much of it at SWUUSI, your super week-long annual gathering, then at Lake Murray, with the largest number of folks, always, from All Souls Church, Tulsa. I had not before been in a District with so much affection, with such a good spirit of forbearance and cooperation among our churches. Sure, there were differences, sharp differences, among ministers and congregations. But here in the Southwest you had well instituted and high expectations for—what our Puritan forebears called—orderly sharing of views and responsibilities.

The results were sometimes stunning. I know one now strong, lively congregation that would likely have remained a weak little group—a "Sunday talking club"—but for SWUUSI. Members of this little fellowship used to tease one of their lay leaders and laugh. "Buddy went to SWUUSI and got religion!" But their whole membership was transformed, over time, by the deeper understanding of the free church Buddy brought home, from having been with more experienced and more committed liberal churchpeople than he had known.

Having come, myself, from a District where there was no institution like SWUUSI, it was clear to me—SWUUSI was the main reason the spirit among Southwest churches was so much better than I was used to. Every year every one of the ministers was there, most with several lay members, with as many as 30 or 40—kids and elders—from All Souls. I had not till then, and have not since, seen that anywhere else, and I've been many times to other UU summer institutes. They have fine features, but none so much affected the spirit among the churches of the region—

because they are not the kind of loyal, lay and ministerial enterprise as SWUUSI.

So I asked, "How did this thing come to be?" The answer was Robert Raible, long-time minister of First Church, Dallas, who retired in 1964. Way back in the late '40s, Robert Raible had kept urging and persuading until he got fixed, set, a pattern of high expectations or, as the Puritans would have said, an orderly rule: All elected ministers will be there with our people from many churches for a seven-day, rich meeting every August, without fail, no excuses accepted. And other ministers, not those he persuaded, still were there every August, without fail, 30 and 35 years later, when I came and when I left. Nowhere written down, this rule was part of the covenant in the Southwest!

And the results showed throughout the region. Why? Because this is a rule of commonsense and natural law: When free churchpeople regularly and freely cooperate—elected leaders and members together, in the spirit of mutual love and in healthy patterns—good happens and keeps on happening, in wider circles. This natural law holds for any association of free churches: We don't get the spirit of mutual love among our scattered and distinct churches, unless our bodies are, regularly, together in the same place—as we are in our home churches, only less often. When elected ministers and members, of a few or many free churches in a region, associate in healthy patterns, all the churches benefit richly.

How do we tell whether our patterns of association are good and helpful, or an awful waste of time, or downright counterproductive, even way off-track? The test: look to what happens in the congregations as a result. See any more vim and vigor, more forbearing engagement and growth in membership, in the congregations? If not, we'd better change our patterns, because our patterns of association matter.

Did you know this? In the 1930s, during the Depression, a third of our New England Unitarian churches died. John Wolf used to boast that in the 1970s, there were more UUs—real live bodies—gathered on Sunday mornings in just the Southwest's five largest churches, than in all New England, where we have many more churches. There's a historical connection in the interdependent web of being between set patterns and spirit and live bodies. It matters how, in what spirit and in what patterns, we do what we do now. And, it's going to matter in future generations.

Often, living participants have no notion how our patterns got started, for the sake of what principles, or to meet which misjudged exigencies, or at the urging of what wise or foolish leaders. But if the patterns are good ones, there's lots of room in them for creativity, varied and innovative response to challenges, and new talent coming on and taking hold. And the churches of a region will thrive. If our patterns are poor, our churches will be corrupted. Instead of giving and taking counsel when differences arise, the people will quarrel viciously and divisively. Or, whole congregations will get stalled in ineptitude and isolation and never learn how to do better.

I name some realities among us: A lot of expensive, time-consuming meetings among various "representatives" of quite differently constituted UU affiliates, not congregations. UUA programs having little if any effect in our churches. An overall church growth rate in 2000 of only .6%, when the population is growing much faster. Almost no ongoing exchange of wise counsel among neighboring churches. Lots of bitter complaint, in print and on the web, about the UUA. Not a few but hundreds of UU congregations stalled in ineptitude and isolation for years. *Something is seriously awry in the patterns of association among our churches.*

I am glad I began learning how to be a UU minister in the Southwest. You set my standards. You were my example of what relations among our free churches can be. So 30 or so years later, I asked for an invitation to give Lectures 5 and 6 of the Minns Lectures here. I hope we can be called to a higher standard of explicitly covenantal patterns among our churches. I figured, if any UUs can understand what I am trying to say, it must be in the Southwest.

I have said we need a critical appreciation of our history, of how our good and poor patterns got set as they did, and a historically informed and inventive imagination, something like Robert Raible's in the 1940s. What is a critical appreciation? Just this: I know you didn't suppose, a minute ago when I was praising Southwest churches, that I left these parts thinking—here there were no problems or deficits. I did not. I never thought everybody here was flawless. I simply saw that your spirit and some of your practices were of a piece. They worked! I was better off for having learned here something more of what is possible among us. A critical appreciation of our past can do the same for us.

Our notions, of what free churches are and could do, always come from concrete human experience, our own or other live people's, or those recorded in history. That's why it's important that, as liberal churchpeople, we not be geographically or temporally parochial. There are things we need to learn from looking at our churches' patterns, set long ago.

A critical appreciation of the Cambridge Platform

So, who were the 17th-century founders of our oldest UU churches? They had been churchpeople in England—many tens of thousands of ordinary members and ministers and University students and professors—appalled, not by all but, by many of the institutional patterns they were born into, in the Church of England. These patterns were already long set before they came to consciousness. But they learned of—what looked to them—very different and much better patterns from history, from the Old and New Testaments of the Bible which they understood as the record books of the free church. Having tried mightily and failed to reform the Church of England—because they were thwarted and persecuted and punished by the kings, the queen and the bishops of England—our ancestors made the amazingly brave and costly choice to remove—some 20,000 of them—to the wilderness of New England in the 1630s. They came to this continent to gather themselves into free churches, in what they called the "liberty of the gospel." These were the churches which in the 19th century first became, on this continent, Unitarian. And we UUs have kept ever since many—not all—of the patterns of free churches, just as they were set in the 17th century.

We could put this way what happened in our UU story, before you and I came into the movie. Our Puritan ancestors left England for New England, not because they disagreed with the Church of England—or other Protestants in Europe—over theology or anthropology—that is, over the nature of God or of humankind. They left because they disagreed over the theology of organization, over the question of how churches ought to be organized in the spirit of mutual love, over who should have authority and why—in churches rooted in that spirit. Two hundred years later, in the early 1800s, when we Unitarians separated from more conservative churches of the Standing Order, the disagreement was over the nature of God and humankind. But we unanimously kept—and have kept to this day—the pattern of covenantal congregational polity set in the 17th century.

There were many more dissenters in England from episcopal polity—control of churches by a hierarchy of bishops—than the 20,000 who came here in the Great Migration of the 1630s. Our folks fervently hoped they might be joined in New England by many more. But the whole scene in England changed drastically in the 1640s with the outbreak there—twice—of civil war, the beheading of Charles I, and the rule of Parliament and Oliver Cromwell as Lord Protector. In all that turmoil, there emerged in Cromwell's army—the guys with weapons—passionately religious advocates for a far more revolutionary, socialist reorganization of the whole society than England was anything like ready for. So, opinion concerning church governance, even among the dissenters from episcopacy, shifted toward presbyterianism—that is, a pattern of authority over the churches, by "representative" bodies, who could deal with any wild-eyed socialist extremists who might spring up in the churches and gain followers within them! (Yes, left-wing political socialism was born in left-wing, independent churches in the 1600s.)

New Englanders were very aware of the shift toward presbyterianism, among their own friends in England, away from New England's scrupulous congregationalism, a pattern in which all religious authority is located in each single, distinct congregation. To deal with all the issues of the Church of England, Parliament called on 109 "divines" and 24 members of Parliament to meet in Winchester Hall in London and agree on what would be the faith and the form of church governance in England. The Assembly began to meet in the summer of 1645, concluded in the fall of 1646, and published the results, the *Winchester Confession of Faith.* Parliament invited two widely respected New England theologians, John Cotton and Thomas Hooker. They did not go because they knew, on the very matter closest to New England hearts, they would now be in a small minority.

So, after publication of the *Winchester Confession*—which included prescription of a presbyterial church order—and at the request of the Massachusetts General Court, the churches sent elected lay and ministerial officers, or "messengers," to convene at Harvard College as the Cambridge Synod. Others could also attend if they wished. This assembly "thought it good to present unto [the local churches], & with them all the churches of Christ abroad, our professed & hearty assent & attestation" to the Winchester Confession, "Excepting only some sections"— namely, those sections having to do with authority in the church, or organization.

That is how we came to have the Cambridge Platform, which consists of a preface and 17 chapters. Each chapter is footnoted with many references to passages from the Scriptures clearly illustrating, to the unanimous satisfaction of the "elders and messengers," that the substance of the congregational way is the same as that of the very first free church, the family of Sarah and Abraham. In our terms they meant—some things have not changed for as long as people have been coming together, either out from under or in the midst of corrupted, hierarchical societies, to live in free groups called churches, whose free and orderly ways are the ways of love, not the coercion of any hierarchy.

Our church ancestors understood the Bible to be mainly about the free and covenanted, social practice of love. They were not, by any means, ignorant of all other history. Their University trained ministers were saturated, especially, with Greek and Roman history. But their periodization of church history they expressed as follows: "The state [of] the members . . . walking in order was either [1] before the law, Oeconomical, that is in families; or [2] under the law, Nation; or [3], since the comming of Christ only congregational. (The term Independent, we approve not.)" [Chapter 2:5]

Paraphrase that. Say that in words we use now. Free churches are groups of people who have covenanted to "walk together"—live together or meet often—in patterned ways, or "in order," in the spirit of mutual love. People have covenanted to do this, over a great stretch of time, first (1) as families, beginning with Sarah and Abraham; then (2) as the nation of ancient Israel, beginning with Moses; and, since the time of Jesus and his disciples, (3) as local congregations. As our forebears understood church history, the holy spirit of mutual love, or the "substance" of a free church—an Aristotelian term—has always been the same, in all three periods. (That is why they found the Old Testament as instructive as the New.) The live gathered bodies of the members are the "matter" of the free church. And its "forme" is the covenantal promise, which defines the membership, determines its organizational shape, or structure, and imbues the church with promise, the potential, to be a life-giving organization for all the larger world.

Again, from the Platform: "The partes of Church-Government are all of them exactly described in [the Scriptures] being parts or means of Instituted worship according to the second Commandment: & therefore continue one and the same. . . ." The "second Commandment" is: "Thou shalt love thy neighbor as thyself." So, our forebears were saying, the substance of the free church is the spirit of neighborly love. And everything in the free church's "administration"—everything—follows naturally and logically from the primacy of this one experienced, central, holy reality, the spirit of neighborly love. In other places in the text this spirit of love is called "the supream power," or Christ, the only head of the church. In the Dedham Church Record, John Allin actually used one X, the Greek letter *chi,* to denote Christ and two XXs to denote the free church, plural Christs, or the spirit of love in live bodies meeting in one place. The one "end," or purpose, of everything the gathered members do, says the Cambridge Platform, is "mutual edification"—that is, mutual learning and teaching concerning the ways of love, one topic with an infinite number of sub-topics since the ways of love are to be sought in all life's complexities. The people must be gathered—meet in the same place at the same time—for mutual learning to take place. Otherwise, the "spirit of love" is just a fuzzy, sentimental head trip, a bodiless abstraction—or as some irreverently say—Sloppy *Agape.*

So, said our forebears, to gather and go about a church's "administration," the members needed three things: (1) *personal experience of the spirit of mutual love between the individual and God,* often described in Puritan sermons as union, or "marriage of the heart," with the spirit of love; (2) to be individually, one by one, called—or drawn—by the spirit of love *to enter the covenant with other members* to love faithfully; and (3) *to elect officers,* lay and ministerial. And there you have—said they—a whole, complete free church in all its "partes," just two "partes," ordinary members and ordinary officers—meaning that free churches have no need, in church affairs, of any higher authorities. Or, as they put it, "[I]t is not left in the power of men, officers, Churches, or any state in the world to add, or diminish, or alter any thing in the least measure therein." [Chapter 1:3]

This formulation eliminates any such thing as the outside supervision or interference of the civil government, or the bishops of an episcopacy, or the authority of any provincial presbyterial body, or—we might add—the UUA board/staff.

A question: Why, since they were patently describing here, independent congregations, did the Cambridge synod "approve not the term Independent"? Because, in the 17th century, those churches which named themselves "Independent" in England had taken the position that whatever happened anywhere else than in each distinct free church was of no concern to them. But in the minds of our congregationalist founders, strong convictions about the autonomy of each church, did not imply sectarian isolation. For they also had, from the Bible, a concept of the church universal—the "Catholick Church"—that great measureless company of people, the living and the dead of every age and land, who have ever experienced and walked in the spirit of mutual love, in whatever church—or no church. They would not make an idol of church organization, even one they believed to be the only right "forme." God was, in their experience, the spirit of mutual love, which hardly justifies "hardness of heart." "[I]s difference about Church-order become the inlett of all the disorders in the kingdom? . . . that we cannot leave contesting & contending about it, till the kingdom be destroyed? . . . [S]urely, either the Lord will cleare up his own will to us, . . . or else we shall learn to bear one another's burdens in a spirit of meekness." [Preface]

Those lines nicely illustrate that strong-minded congregationalists can certainly see the need for and plead for tolerance, as 17th-century Puritans did in regard to many matters, though not in as many as we wish they had.

But even more emphatically did the independence of free churches *not* mean isolation from other free churches, according to the Cambridge Platform. Though all churches were "distinct . . . & therefore have no dominion over one another," they are to be a *community* of independent churches. They were to "take thought for one another's wellfare." "[W]hen any church wanteth light or peace among themselves it is a way of communion . . . to meet together . . . to consider and argue the point in doubt or difference; and, having found out the way of truth and peace, to recommend the same . . . to the churches whom the same may concern."

It was not acceptable "if a church be rent with divisions . . . and yet refuse to consult with other churches for healing. . . ." If a divided church does refuse to "consult," neighboring churches—not a staffperson from headquarters—neighboring churches are to "exercise a fuller act of communion by way of admonition." That is, free churches are not to regard the challenging difficulties in congregational life—either their own or others'—as none of anybody else's business. Rather each is to listen to other churches' counsel. "[S]o may one church admonish another, and yet without usurpation. . . ." [Chapter 15]

In all times it is a good thing, said our founders, if members of two or several churches—all the members—occasionally come together. A church with two ministers should lend one to a congregation whose minister is ill. When members move, even temporarily, to another town, the church should send a letter of recommendation to the congregation in that town. In case of need, one church should furnish another with officers, or sometimes money. And by all means, neighboring churches should help a new church get started well and rightly. If any one church gets too large to meet all in one place, some of the members should form a new congregation, "[a]s bees, when the hive is too full, issue out by swarms, and are gathered into other hives. . . ."

A question: Did they really get all this from the Bible? They really thought they did. It is fascinating to read the closely reasoned argument of the Platform, which often uses the terminology of Aristotelian and Ramist logic, and look up, as you read, the many biblical passages footnoted in every paragraph. What you see is—they read the Bible with a very different interpretive key than you or I might use. The books of the Bible are mostly, of course, not lists of rules, but poems, lyrics of hymns, strung-together pieces of the prophets' sermons and narratives, stories of events. But our 17th-century congregationalists were obsessed with issues

93

of authentic authority. So they read every word of the Bible asking of the texts, "What was decided here? Whose counsel was sought? Who decided? Which people had to be involved if a decision was to be considered legitimate? What did people in these stories do if they disagreed?" They then inferred that answers to these questions were to be taken as illustrating the rules of authentic authority in free churches.

An example: An elected officer in our oldest churches was called the "ruling elder." An ordained lay member, he was primarily responsible for "discipline"—that is, for talking privately, tenderly but firmly, with any member whose ways of behaving were not ways of the spirit of love. Consider an event in one our churches. Suppose an angry member starts loudly saying harsh things about what the RE Committee and teachers have carefully chosen to teach in a church school class? I've been in weak churches, scared to death that anyone might resign. Some RE folks would dump a curriculum in a minute, to avoid a fuss with one viciously rude person who had no understanding of what the teachers were trying to do or why. They put in its place a bland, uncontroversial curriculum. Then some families quit coming because the kids said church school was boring! By whatever name, "ruling elders" provide a better response to any members' unruly anger than church-lite! That better response is the work of free church discipline.

Once, a super UU couple joined a church I served. They came every Sunday, but without their middle school kids. So I said one day, 'Where are the kids?" Well, the parents' work had required them to move often. And three times, after a move, the kids went to a new church school class doing a unit on the Hopi Indians. So these kids decided UU churches are weird. Fixated on the Hopis. They wouldn't come to ours!

Our earliest free churches elected and ordained the "ruling elder" to deal with such as that first harsh member. If the member refused to listen, even when, later, two or three others members could not persuade him or her to listen either, the ruling elder took the issue to the whole church. All the members together decided whether a reprimand, or even dismissal, was in order. The "ruling elder" couldn't just pronounce, by himself, on any issue; authentic authority lay in the whole gathered congregation. The model for both the office and the "rule" of the "ruling elder" they took from one of Jesus' sermons in the Gospel according to Matthew.

But "discipline" was not solely the ruling elder's responsibility, even to initiate. *Every* member should speak candidly to any member whose ways were unloving. This "rule" they inferred from a story about Paul in the book of Acts. Paul, though he had no authority over Peter, told Peter, in front of the whole church, that it was wrong of him to refuse to eat with the Gentile members at church suppers.

But for all their reverence for the Scriptures, there is, in the Platform, a rather impatient-sounding admission that not every "necessary circumstance" of the free church is clearly indicated by some biblical passage. If any procedures should seem only practical, or "necessary," two tests of reason were to be applied: (1) Is their "end" "unto edification"? And (2) "in respect to the manner," are these things to be done "decently, and in order, according to the nature of the things them selves *& Civil and Church Custom*. [D]oth not even nature it selfe teach you? [Y]ea they are in some sort determined particularly, . . . so, *if there bee no errour* . . . concerning their determination, the determining of them is to be accounted *as if it were divine*." [emphasis added; Chapter 1:4]

Well, let it be said at once, some of the worst mistakes our founders made—very costly to later generations—were precisely those patterns they "accounted as if [they] were divine," when, for all their careful reasoning and logic, they were merely habits "of Civil and Church Custom," very bad cultural habits, brought from Europe, which they ought never to have continued here, not because Bible stories contain no precedent for them, but because they would work ill in the long run. These practices were "determined," not in accordance with the "substance" of the free churches,—the spirit of mutual love—but in accordance with an authoritarian expedient of coercion.

Money is certainly "necessary" for churches, whose mission of "edification"—teaching and learning—is needed by and beneficial to the whole town, or parish—they called it—in which the church was located. So, our ancestors concluded, it is perfectly reasonable that the magistrates, as they had done in England, should coerce all landowning citizens to pay the parish rate, taxes, to support free churches—that is, churches properly constituted according to the Cambridge Platform. So, while the laws of New England didn't forbid organization of churches not part of the Standing Order, members of these other churches—including our Universalist ancestors—had the very devil of a time getting an exemption from also supporting, with their taxes, the legally designated "free churches."

And who fought hardest to maintain the "necessary" rule of tax support for the *right* free churches in the 1830s in Massachusetts? Why, the Unitarian heirs of the Puritans. So, why did all those New England Unitarian churches die in the 1930s? Because, after they lost Massachusetts public tax support in 1834, Unitarian churches were heavily dependent financially for the next 100 years on a few wealthy members or "pew owners." When these few lost their money in the Great Depression of the 1930s, a third of our churches collapsed. *Church patterns matter and have long effect, for good and for ill.*

Another mistake of our founders: Early in the text, the Cambridge Platform makes about as strong a statement on the importance of the covenant as one can imagine. Only each member's promise, made freely and one by one—to walk together with other members in the ways of love—makes the people a free church. "[It] followeth, it is not faith in the heart, nor the profession of that faith, nor cohabitation, nor Baptisme: 1) Not faith in the heart? becaus that is invisible: 2) not a bare profession; because that declareth them no more to be members of one church then of another: 3) not Cohabitation; Atheists or Infidels may dwell together with believers: 4) not Baptism . . . , as circumcision in the old Testament, which gave no being unto the church, the church being before it, & in the wilderness without it." [Chapter 4:5]

I say, "Great! Wonderful!" But then, in Chapter 12, titled "On Admission of members . . . ," are sentences like these: "[S]uch as are admitted therto, as members, ought to be examined & tryed first; whether they be fit & meet to be received. . . . [T]hey must profess & hold forth in such sort, as may satisfie rational charity that [repentance and faith] are there indeed. . . . A personall & publick confession, & declaring of Gods manner of working upon the soul, is bothe lawfull, expedient, & usefull, in sundry respects, & upon sundry grounds."

This part of the Platform makes me want to cuss. When new people are thinking of joining a free church, those already members need to be "examined and tryed." It is the members' obligation, I say, to explain—in very simple and appealing words—what is so fine about the covenant of their free church and warmly to invite others to enter it with them. If members cannot explain what their covenant is and what it means, that church is not "fit & meet" to be joined! I said in Lecture 3, I think we need to be empathetic with our earliest congregational ancestors' concept of salvific spiritual experience. And it's only fair to add, if we had seen what they saw, what an awful institution the Church had become in their time, maybe we, too, would have thought the best hope, of keeping their churches from morphing back to horrible hierarchy, was to keep them "pure." But this horrible requirement for membership—that old members test and judge the substance of new members' neighborly love—soon gave the founders and their children no end of trouble, starting in the 1650s, only a decade after they wrote the Platform. But it's not much comfort that they suffered for it. For this dreadful mistake is the main historical reason we liberals almost forgot the covenant 300 years later, in the 20th century.

Here's what happened. The founders tied entering the covenant to a very special kind of experience, an ecstatic "falling in love with God." But even in the second generation, most people never had that ecstatic experience. So, in the 18th century, preachers like Jonathan Edwards and other "revivalists" thought they had to make this thing happen, with hell-fire and brimstone preaching of a sort which would have horrified the 17th-century Puritans. The covenant then became linked, in liberals' minds, with 18th-century "revivalism." Thus, our 19th-century liberal churches kept the old, earliest covenants on the books—beautiful, simple promises to walk together in the ways of love, but the covenant was mostly not talked about. This bad pattern works ill yet today.

For if you don't talk about the covenant—the members' basic agreement, the simple promise that constitutes the church as a church, the promise all who will are cordially invited to enter with us—what *do* you say is the basis of a liberal church? A creed? Tens of thousands of liberals have never been able to respond to that question any better than by saying, "Oh, no! No. Not a creed! We don't believe in creeds." You know the question which follows that empty negation: "Then what do Unitarian Universalists believe?"

Will the day ever come when many, many of us can say, *Ours is a covenantal church. We join by promising one another that we will be a beloved community, meeting together often to find the ways of love, as best we can see to do. We have found there's always more to learn about how love really works, and could work, in our lives and in the world.* I hope that day comes.

One more mistake of our founders: Our founders, ready as they were to defy the kings and bishops of England to establish free churches, nevertheless assumed that tiered levels of privilege and authority in society—and in the churches—were "natural." So, the Platform said the free church had a "mix't government." "Kingship" of the holy spirit of Christ made the free church a "monarchy." And because the members elected, and could dismiss, their own officers, the free church was also a "democracy." But then, since the members were to "obey" their officers, once elected, the "elders"—elected ministers and lay officers whom we call board members—were the "aristocracy."

My response to that is: What a crock! Members not elected to any office in our earliest churches could be, and often were, anything but "obedient," if they didn't agree with their "aristocracy." Even if the members got talked into adopting some measure by their "elders," if they really didn't approve it, they just wouldn't do it, no matter how often they were "admonished" to do it. Phony democracy worked then as now, when our members, year after year, do nothing with all those "study issues" we keep "democratically" voting to take up, these "votes" really involving very few members. Most of our members don't agree that these issues are well handled in this poor pattern. And the many admonitions of our "aristocracy" can't get the members of our free churches to "do it," either.

But it is simply a fact that nearly all colonial and later New Englanders—of all classes—assumed, for a long time, that status once acquired is status deserved in perpetuity. So, a pattern early developed that lasted, among Unitarians, into the late 20th century. Once officers were elected in the earliest churches, and—in our lifetimes—once people were just appointed to some position in the AUA or the UUA, unless they did something really awful, ministers and lay leaders tended to stay in office a long time and pass their status on to their children. The same was true, from the beginning, of civil offices in New England towns and in the legislature. Connections and influence then, often, led to wealth.

So, rather quickly, New England developed something like a European aristocracy, a class, economically and politically privileged by birth. Many members of our earliest-named Unitarian churches—after 200 years in the Standing Order and named Unitarian in the 19th century—were of this class, directly related to old patterns of privilege in their churches and State. There are advantages to a culture in having a well-educated and wealthy class, but in the long run patterns of assumed privilege work ill. Without new leaders, without fresh connections and language—fresh words of abiding truth—churches get stale, complacent, dull and stuck. Then, trying to wake the people up—develop new leadership, start new programs and bring in new members—is like pulling whales' teeth. Established authority figures don't like it and they will resist needed change mightily.

Trouble is, of course, if there's no way to get leaders off elevated boards and staffs except to mount an insurrection and have a big fight. Even "free" churches are not free to do anything but creak along, blindly repeating the same boring, counterproductive, set pattern of mistakes working ill in the churches. This old pattern—of regarding "leaders" as an "aristocracy," or leaving programming decisions to "leadership at the highest continental level"—has proved a bad pattern of organization, for all of us. We have kept variations of it way too long. Ultimately, in the long run, "leaders" of this type can't get members of free churches to do diddly squat.

I trust you see that I have hardly gone ga-ga over our flawless 17th-century founders, though I have come to love them. Courageous, intelligent, brilliant even, creative and right on about many things, they failed to see the consequences of their share of mistaken assumptions. The love in their hearts and the human capacity to reason about and learn together the ways of love, they rightly saw as divine gifts. Yet, they also believed it was fine to take their reasoning about practical, "necessary circumstances" as divine "if there bee no errour!" A rather large "if," you and I would say. But then, of all the changes between the 17th century and our lifetimes, the greatest may be our learning—given all the ghastly tragedies of the 20th century—that human reasoning often fails the test of time. That doesn't mean we shouldn't use our heads! It means we need to be humble about the fact that the best of us tend to institutionalize patterns we think are only "practical," when these poor patterns are nothing but a convenience to some, forms of governance working ill in our liberal free churches, even now.

If the Platform authors were over-confident that, with close enough attention to logic and rules, they could find *the* truth, we need to remember—in that, they were quite at one with the spirit of their age. The 17th century was a time of great scientific discovery and doctrinaire belief in certain circles that the logical, mathematical discoveries of Newton, for example, certainly heralded our coming acquisition of the absolute truth about everything. The Puritans were not the only ones in their time—or later—to be rather awfully sure of themselves.

How much more, then, do we need to remind ourselves, that unrecognized and false assumptions characteristic of our time—such as the notion that the nonprofit corporation pattern of board/staff governance is "natural" for our Association—must be part of who we are, too. It is terribly arrogant to suppose that because we can see, with hindsight, mistakes of the generations before us, it's okay to demonize them. Without demonizing them, we need to be as clear as we can be about their gifts to us and their mistakes, because the consequences of both still shape us.

Then we can try to answer, not ever flawlessly but better than we have, the questions: What reclaimed patterns of governance might be good for us, especially in our ways of associating as liberal free congregations in our time? Could we invent patterns based in the spirit of neighborly love among our churches, for our time, appropriate in our society? In Lecture 6 I'll try my hand at those questions.

Lecture 6: Toward a Covenanted Association of Congregations: On Patterns of Authentic Authority among Free Churches

I'd like us to look at the mix of meanings carried these days by one little word. What does it mean, for example, when a church member, on coming back home, is asked by another who didn't go, "How was SWUUSI this year?" And the response is, "It was *super.*"

Suppose you are asked if you know a certain UU in Texas, and you say, "Oh, he's a *super* guy."

Suppose you are on the nominating committee of your church. The name of a certain young woman comes up, and somebody says, "I don't know how she does so much. She defines the term '*super* mom.'"

I couldn't go last month to our church's annual meeting. Joe went. When he got home, I asked, "How'd it go?" He said the meeting room was so full some members had to stand. Even so, they voted on five complex issues in less than an hour. On one secret-ballot issue, whether to be a "Welcoming Congregation," the vote was 93% in favor, and except for two abstentions, the yes vote on the four other motions was unanimous! Members gave our outgoing president a long, standing ovation. In a challenging year she has been a *super* lay officer. Adjourned, the members were laughing and hugging all over the place. It was a *super* meeting of a *super* church.

With reference to people we talk about *super* athletes or entertainment stars. But we also use this word to describe material things and other enterprises as common as churches. A friend eager to tell you about a recent purchase could say, "I got a *super* deal on it at TomDick'n'Harry's *super*market."

Look at all the different realities we are talking about here! A week-long gathering of our religious folk; an individual; a short annual meeting; a high performer in sport or music; a material thing somebody bought; and a store. See then. Our word *super*, applied to all these realities just means—quite good. But what a variety of goods! At least five very different goods: the rich quality of worship services and workshops and play at a super SWUUSI; the easy decency of a super guy; the efficiency of people who do well, even with many competing demands on their time; the prices at a store; or the striking abilities of a famous few way off somewhere, not here where we ordinary people are. That's a long list of meanings for one little word.

Note two other possible meanings of *super*, not present in these examples. In not one was there a hint of anything *supernatural*, that is, alien to or out of the range of the everyday. Even super athletes and entertainers only manifest unusual, extraordinary abilities, not abilities ordinary people don't have at all. Even I can shoot baskets and sing, just not as well as Michael Jordan or Sarah Brightman.

Also not present in these examples, was any hint of hierarchical control, as when we might say, "Doubting Tom doesn't believe in us. He thinks he has to *supervise* everything we do." No. In all the earlier examples of typical UU conversation, the talk was about the actions of free people, these actions manifesting certain everyday living patterns, which evoke, from other free people, a spontaneously offered assessment—super.

You may know that the Latin word *super* means "over" or "above," though in our usage it hardly ever has that connotation, at all. Imagine some Latin specialist, a few centuries from now—say in 2401—making a study of the "old" North American Unitarian Universalist movement of the late 20th–early 21st centuries, and concluding—from the fact that we often describe things as super—that in this "dark" age, UUs fell into gross superstition!

That could be someone's conclusion in a later era, for lack of knowing a really simple linguistic fact of all eras: the meanings of words change, sometimes very quickly. I remember when little corner grocery stores first began to be replaced by supermarkets, after World War II. They seemed to me as a kid so grand! But in just a few years supermarkets were as common as corner groceries had been. And soon, we starting describing all sorts of ordinary quite good things as super. But anybody not living in our times could not know what we mean by super without what literary critics call a close reading of our usage in the context of our times.

I trust I'm making sense. But why begin a lecture titled "Toward a Covenanted Association of Congregations" by looking at the mix of meanings among us of this little word?

I wanted to start this way because we liberals can sometimes be really dense in our reading of other eras of our own free-church tradition. Actually, we derive from a history of free churchpeople who spent their lives in constructive opposition to unfreedom in their times—as do we in ours. But we can get so hung up on what we take to be the meanings of traditional words that we can't read our own church history. In earlier eras our people have used different words for our super, or quite good. For example, our 17th-century ancestors—from whom we inherited congregational polity—simply meant by "the liberty of the gospel"—the freedom of loving good people to gather, unsupervised, in free churches and to associate freely, without supervision, in a community of free churches.

We may say of members of our free churches now—they are super people. People of this very same ilk our ancestors called "saints." By that term they just meant quite good people, super people. And by their term "communion of churches" they just meant a quite good community of free churches, or what we call our Association of Congregations.

The meanings of words change, all the time. But some realities do not change in human history. The reality and the ways of liberty in religiously rooted free-church communities do not change. What our ancestors named the holy spirit of Christ, we liberals now name the spirit of life or love or truth. They meant by their term the same crucial reality—of heart and mind and body—we mean by ours.

In the Cambridge Platform our founders took great care to make it clear that they were only talking there about ordinary free-church members and the members' ordinary leaders, their locally elected officers. They said the free church records show that, in the whole centuries-long free-church tradition, there have been only a few unelected, extraordinary leaders: Moses, David, Jesus and the twelve apostles. They said in our church bodies now, we don't have any extraordinary leaders, just ordinary. So it is with us. When we talk about super free churches—what they called gathered saints—we're only talking about the doings of ordinary people in our liberally religious bodies which—without any outside supervision, and at our ordinary best—are pretty darned fine.

But wait a minute! If the covenantal, congregational polity of ordinary free church members and ordinary officers was the whole subject of the Cambridge Platform, who were these unelected extraordinary leaders of ages past, and why were they brought into the discussion?

I'll try explaining this way. Don't we have in our churches now some informal leaders, our "wise old heads," not currently elected to any office, but so beloved and respected for their wisdom and insight, that we fairly often—thank God!—heed their counsel, especially when we get into a dispute? Often quietly, in the midst of a heated and confusing argument, one of our unelected "wise old heads" rises to say something like this: "Well, I think we'd better not do 'x', or 'y' and 'z' are apt to follow. And, I think, if we want 'c' to happen, we'd better first do 'a' and 'b'."

And all the members meeting say, "Oh, yeah! Right. Of course." The heat and argument blow over, and we get on with making a decision that we all think is quite good—super.

All healthy free churches have unelected leaders like this. They are our prophets, in Hebrew, the *nabi*. They are our informally acknowledged "wise heads," though not currently, or even ever, elected. Some are not even "old" but rich anyhow with wisdom.

But every once in a very long while—according to our founders' reading of the free-church tradition—a few extraordinary "officers" have arisen and spoken in the midst of some historic, long continued, heated and confusing argument. These few had not been even informal leaders, much less elected. These few extraordinary prophets just arose and spoke, with such transparently authentic authority that many members were amazed at the simplicity of obvious truth. They said, "Well, of course, that's true. Why didn't we think of that? That's clearly what we should do and how."

And what did these few, whom the Cambridge Platform called extraordinary "officers," have in common? Just this: words spoken by these unelected prophets were so persuasive, to great numbers of then living free churchpeople, that—three different times in history—the free congregations changed their whole set of "bylaws," or patterns of governance. They then adopted new patterns of free church governance, though always—crucially—keeping the same "substance" of any free church of any time—the spirit of mutual love, for one another and for their role in making their whole society more loving and just—through their own doings of love.

So—our congregational New England ancestors reasoned—since the free churches never elected these extraordinary prophets, of such extraordinary power to persuade free people, God elected them. In these few cases the people didn't even have opportunity—as John Allin of our Dedham church put it—to become "acquainted with their (spiritual) tempers and guifts." Nor in these few cases was there anything like a nominating committee, a search committee or candidating for election. These prophets just started speaking; free churches listened, and then changed their whole way of "administration," the way free churches do governance.

Or, as we might put it now, their clearly voiced insights made these extraordinary prophets a powerfully persuasive *voice of the situation*—that is, the situation of any religious people wanting to be free and loving and wise together, without supervision. There you have, right in the Cambridge Platform, a *natural theology of special revelation!* In our time we say, this sort of thing has happened among peoples of other traditions, too! Because in certain crucial ways, human nature is the same in all traditions, however these traditions vary in other important ways.

In Moses' time the free congregations broke the pattern of isolated family style churches and called themselves a nation, Israel—meaning that to make decisions affecting the whole nation, elders from all the congregations met and took counsel till they concurred. In David's time the governance of this free-church-nation became a monarchy, in theory dependent on God's "anointing of his Son" for the throne. There followed David, though, a long series of kings whose ways—the prophets kept declaring—did not much resemble the ways of the King of the Universe.

In that long period the prophets of the congregations made the most noise and voiced the harshest criticism. Then, finally, in Roman times, Jesus and the Apostles arose and spoke. As a consequence, many free churches shucked nationalism and became again family-style congregations, only this time, of every ethnic background in the Mediterranean world, not of one nation.

Our 17th-century congregational ancestors reclaimed key and crucial elements of the free church tradition. Sadly—for us—they did not see the "nationalism" of their ties with the Treasury of the Commonwealth of Massachusetts, or other continuing patterns of church leadership they adopted, as wrong. These "practical" patterns—so long kept—proved quite impractical and worked ill in the long run, among us. By the end of the 20th century we, their liberal heirs, did not have many liberal and quite good—super—free churches. According to the UUA board minutes of June 2000, more than a third—389—of our thousand or so churches have 60 or fewer members. Almost another third—325—have more than 60 but fewer than 160. Only 25 have more than 800 members. We can't do much good in the world in such small numbers as that.

So what is our problem—as liberal free congregations—now? I'm not even going to say I believe; I *know* with all my head and heart—we UUs are just as loving and hungry to be faithfully loving people, and just as gifted, as intelligent, as hard working and as good as any ordinary people who ever lived, the only kind that have ever lived, in any time. Why, then, do we have so many weak churches, churches and fellowships not thriving, not growing, not going anywhere, not doing much? Of course, we have bright lights, spread across the vast North American continent. And of course, the health of churches is not a function of number, but spirit and patterns of living and doing. Always, some of our churches, large and small, have been and are super.

But, friends, you can't keep a spirited, lively liberal church from growing unless it's located someplace where there aren't any people! So why do we not have more, many more spirited, thriving liberal churches full of people? Have we lost something from our tradition, or forgotten something very important? Are we quite good super people doing things we don't see as wrong, that work ill among us, to the world's loss?

106

I guess you have guessed my answer. *We've got the locus of authority wrong in our Association.* In our UUA we have gradually turned many authority issues on their heads, topsy-turvy. But I am also sure of this: A lot of harsh criticism of the UUA will not help us become a thriving Association! I dare say the great Hebrew prophets in the time of Israelite kings spent too much time fussing and threatening extinction. Amos, for example, fussed hard about the meaningless assemblies the free churches had every year in his time, and the smell of burnt offerings—resources burnt up and wasted on expensive feasts and shows—with nothing to show from these mass assemblies in the poor neighborhoods of the nation.

Without fussing, if I can I want to try to show you a simple vision of many covenanted congregations freely and richly associating in neighborly ways throughout the UUA. I even hope you might say, "Let's covenant to do it."

Where this vision of covenanted congregations came from

First, I have to ask what you know about our UUA Extension Program. In case you don't know much, I'll just tell you that I was an "extension" minister before the Program began and after I was technically out of it. The vision I want to offer you comes from what I learned in 20 years of working with our congregations, ranging in size from about 40 to about 250 members, two brand-new ones and six a generation or two old. I learned first-hand and very personally about nearly every kind of trouble ordinary officers and members of our liberal free churches can get into, and also about some UUA staffpeople whom we should never appoint to positions that can be so easily, and secretly, abused. At least I pray there aren't many more kinds of free-church troubles than I learned about. Here I just list the troubles I walked into the middle of as an "extension" minister:

- The terrible after-effects of ministers and members who didn't know when to keep their pants buttoned at the waist.
- Naive ministers and lay officers who had no idea how to help our members build or re-build a healthy church.

- Onerous and foolish debts a series of church boards handled very poorly.
- Ridiculously low pledging.
- Lay leaders who said they wanted to change and grow and really didn't, who fought, tooth and nail, once their church began to change and grow, to keep it small.
- Leaking, rotting and underinsured buildings.
- A fire which destroyed a poorly wired building.
- Custodians and members who never happened onto the word "clean."
- Prosperous non-member groups, larger in numbers than our membership, who used our buildings for such wildly low user fees that these prosperous non-church groups were, in fact, generously subsidized out of our churches' small budgets.
- Lay members sure they could preach, who couldn't.
- Teens whose lives were in ruins from hard drugs, two teens dead of drug use and another in prison.
- A District executive who secretly pledged permanently to block any UUA funds from ever coming to a promising new congregation, if the members called a certain minister that a neighboring UU minister feared would draw off his members.
- The collusion of UUMA chapter officers with that District executive to see that he got away with this secret corruption of our covenantal, congregational polity.
- Two other UUA staffpeople who ignored elected officers and instead, strengthened the hands of two congregations' least able, most destructive unelected leaders, thus stalling both congregations in trouble they had been working their way out of, for several more years.
- And more and more bad, futile stuff like that, not exactly the sort of thing you ever hear about at our District meetings or General Assemblies as presently structured, or read about in the *UU World*.

Hear me now, please. With all these different and difficult problems, every congregation I served as minister had two things in common.

First, in every single small or mid-size Unitarian Universalist congregation stuck in trouble, I found numerous super people, young and old, our very own liberal saints under trial. Wonderful, splendid people who keep our covenant. They don't run. They will not desert our slowly dying churches. They keep trying, in the spirit of mutual love, doing the best they can see to do, no matter how mediocre and sad and dysfunctional things get. Why? Because they remember better days from the past, or they have a notion of excellence they brought from another UU church, or something. Somehow, they have a vision of the fine reality their church could be. And so they are there, every week, year in and year out, smiling, singing, hoping, waiting in faith. They keep our covenant alive.

And here's the second thing all our weak and troubled congregations have in common: *isolation.* Not from the general population. These churches are all in areas thick with people. They are isolated from other Unitarian Universalist congregations! In not a single one of them did the members even know, or ever counsel with, members of other nearby UU churches, within only two or three hours or less driving distance. How far is that today? I know people who commute two hours, to and from work, every day!

These congregations got me to come work with them—though not all through "official" channels—because they are all members of our Association. But not one—in my 20 years with them—ever got any freely-offered, neighborly counsel from members of any neighboring UU congregation.

Why? Because we UUs have forgot how to be just ordinary, quite good neighboring congregations. We've forgot what it means freely to associate among our own free churches, except through some extra-congregational, title-or-committee-ridden "District" or "the UUA"—entities we describe as over us—or some affiliate organization, some of these being "super" in the worst sense of that word, not in our everyday sense of "quite good."

If you good UUs listening have never, as officers or members of your church, done anything just plain neighborly with other UU congregations, I'm not accusing you of dereliction. I am confessing. I'm as bad as we all are in this. In 20 years I thought of asking one ordinary lay member of a neighboring church to come and counsel with leading lay members, exactly twice. The help these two laypeople freely gave us was wonderful. Beyond that, I never thought to ask for help, and no UU neighbors ever thought to offer it. God help us! The wonder is not that our "movement" is so small. The wonder is that we are still here! Maybe we are still here only because of our isolated saints!

Poor patterns we have "grown" in our formal UUA

Here I offer an analysis of how we UUs have slid into poor governance patterns in our UUA, without really thinking together of what we've been doing. Then I'll try to show you how our congregations could actually be transformed, in not too long a time, simply and with far less expenditure of time and money than we now spend with very little to show for it. We have not even grown enough to get back up the number of members we had in our churches in 1968—a generation ago.

In our free churches authentic authority resides in decisions made by the members of each congregation. We're all agreed on that. Members elect each congregations' officers—ministers and board members, ordained and lay. But we have fallen into a very bad pattern of Association governance. Members elect "delegates" to District meetings and GAs, who vote there or by absentee ballot, to elect officers of our Association. But in most congregations most of the time, "election" of these "delegates" is strictly *pro forma*. Most members either don't know about or don't care about these "delegate" elections; so we just rubber stamp as our "choice" whoever happens to have the time or interest or money to go. And this is how we have got, in practice, a phony democracy.

What have we done? We have put authority to elect the officers of our Association carelessly, casually into the hands of people who may or may not have much wisdom, much understanding of covenantal congregational polity, or even any deep involvement with our local congregations! For a long time, we have hardly considered whether these "delegates" do or do not have these needed qualifications for making such decisions.

So, "delegates" elected *pro forma* elect the UUA board and president. These latter then appoint a jillion committees which local members never heard of, and appoint staffpeople who appoint other staffpeople who appoint other staffpeople.

So, the only power to do what counts in our Association—design and administer programs for our congregations' optional use—winds up in the hands of appointees appointed by appointees—some of whom retain their offices for decades—these appointed by UUA officers, elected by "delegates," elected only *pro forma* by our congregations! UUA elections get more complicated and expensive every go-round, even while some, who care deeply, wonder why "the UUA" puts out programs that members of congregations won't use—or if we do, many complain bitterly about. And we wonder why our congregations are so uninterested in "affairs" of the UUA. What do we mean when we speak of "the UUA"? We mean about 150 people on the board, the staff, certain appointed committees plus the officers of certain "affiliated" organizations. These folks are awfully busy doing something, but their doings seem to most of us to have little to do with matters that matter on the congregational "level." Do you not often hear this talk of "levels?" Three levels: "Highest" is the continental, "UUA" level. District boards and committees are "mid-level." What happens in our congregations is on the lowest "level."

This year as many as 40 Canadian congregations may withdraw from the UUA. Many reasons have been recently put forward on the internet. I think by far the most cogent of them was given by a Canadian minister, Mac Elrod. Someone had said that if Canadian churches withdraw, they will no longer have "input" into UUA RE programs they will still use after separation.

Mac responded, "We have had very little success in getting Canadian content into UUA programmes and curricula. For the first time the UUA is agreeing as part of the Accord [the proposed separation agreement] to relax copyright so that Canadian substitutions can be made for American references, [to] U.S. tax laws, quotations of the U.S. [political documents], references affected by our differing medical and criminal justice systems, as well as a differing racial pattern, bilingualism, and multi-culturalism."

Sadly, our Canadian "delegates" to General Assemblies have been voicing for years unheeded complaints of UUA board/staff inflexibility

111

and of programs not appropriate to their needs, not to mention the hours at GAs spent on resolutions aimed at the U.S. Congress. But these Canadian complaints are only different in focus, not in kind, from the same sort of complaints concerning rigidly prescribed procedures for raising capital funds and certain narrowly-conceived—but insisted-upon—adult education materials.

But our overall picture is still worse. UUs are quite good at organizing out in the world around specific social issues. That's one of our great strengths. Thousands of our members do responsible and super social action in these organizations. But our UUA board grants UUA affiliate status to all kinds of independently organized groups—not congregations. Unhappily, boards and staff of these affiliates now constantly work to influence decisions of the UUA board/staff. This pattern is so pervasive we seem at times more like an Association of UUA Board/Staff and Affiliates than an Association of Congregations!

I need to be clear here. Some of these groups do marvelous work. I have belonged and contributed to many of them. I was president of one for four years. But our pattern of Association governance has gone far awry when UUA Officers pay more attention to these affiliate boards and their staffpeople than to elected officers of member congregations. Affiliate programs completely dominate General Assemblies. The GA Planning Office will help any affiliate group arrange for two hour-long programs each, and an exhibition booth to promote their projects, some of which are miles from anything members at home would recognize as having to do with matters that matter in our congregations. GAs have become fairs, very, very expensive annual weeks of hoopla and propaganda. Many District patterns are no more helpful in our churches. All this is the product of phony democracy. These patterns are every one of them inefficient, a waste of precious time and energy, and sterile, fruitless with reference to the world's need for more thriving liberal free churches.

How could we make the UUA better?

We could make a few bylaw changes and change for the better the whole character of our Association.

We currently list as our first principle "the inherent worth and dignity of every person." This does not mean we assume every person has grown equally in wisdom. Question: What do we cherish as most holy in our common life as congregations? Answer: The power of loving and reasoning persuasion, in the midst of ongoing dialogue among gathered members, to reveal to us what we together find to be those right and worthy acts we ought and need and want to do, in the spirit of mutual love. This is our theology of free-church governance. This is what it means to believe in "deeds not creeds." This is what it means for members of a free church to be in covenant with one another to find together and then *do* acts matching our dignity and worth as free churchpeople.

So, when we elect officers in our congregations, the issue is: Who among us has the wisdom and skill, in the dialogue of our religious community, to help us learn together, what would be good for us to do. In free churches the only power we grant to leaders is the power of persuasion.

So, the first principle of our *Association* needs to be our common faith in the inherent worth and dignity of *every free congregation*—specifically, our faith in our members' power to elect wise, insightful officers, lay and ordained. For a thriving Association can be based in nothing other than our faith in every member congregation's capacity to be a quite good, super congregation. Ordained and lay officers of our member congregations—elected directly, not *pro forma*—are best qualified to elect officers of our UUA. We need to change our UUA bylaws to replace "delegates" with *officers* of our churches.

This change would be resisted by our many GA and District "buffs" who have attended these meetings as delegates, year after year. Some of these "buffs" are wonderful, informal leaders at home, not currently elected, but beloved and respected Wise Heads, whose wisdom—thank God!—we often heed at home. But we also have far too many District and GA "junkies"—folks hooked on the false prestige of "titles," organizational "insiderism" and crowds. Many of these "junkies" are seldom there in our congregations. And currently, we get too many UUA "leaders" from among District and GA "junkies" who think *they* know, better than our congregations, what "the UUA" should be doing. Some of them even define "leadership" as being out "in front" on issues our poor benighted churches just don't "get"!

Several advantages would soon follow from empowering our congregations' officers to elect UUA officers: (1) UUA officers would have a much clearer sense of who it is they are accountable to—officers of congregations, accountable to members.

(2) If we had more UUA votes in fewer meetings of our lay officers currently serving congregations—along with our ministerial officers—we would soon have a UUA much more effective in strengthening our churches. For our elected church officers know what our congregations really need and want the UUA to do. Ministerial officers already have a vote in District and GA Meetings. We should have long ago so honored and empowered our lay officers. For our most crucial votes, every year, are cast in congregational meetings, when we elect our lay officers.

(3) Locating UUA authority in the hands of our locally elected lay officers would do much to clarify our understanding of free church governance. As things stand, we keep confusing the governance of free churches with the government of a free nation, two very, very different institutional realities. As citizens of a free nation, we elect representatives to speak for us and to enact laws, which the government, then, has the power legally to coerce citizens to obey. In the governance of free churches, no "representatives" speak for the members. Congregational governance attends to a holy, ever-moving dynamic of local power—the power of loving, reasoning persuasion—on which we stake the very life of our churches. Free churches only live by the power of the free spirit of mutual love, working in our own minds and hearts, with no coercion and no law, save the natural laws of human nature and of all that is holy, these laws not enacted by any legislature.

(4) With a simple change in our bylaws—and practice—we could make our UUA, for the first time, a covenanted association. We could change our bylaws to say that membership in our Association means: Our congregations' officers shall meet annually for a few days to take counsel together concerning the overall life and health of our congregations and our common needs. Each member congregation will every year send to this meeting at least one elected lay officer currently serving, all other

elected officers being welcome and urged to attend as well. Our annual meetings will always be open to any members of our member congregations, but only elected officers shall address the assembly or vote.

In any covenant there's got to be a *there* there, or there is no covenant. The covenant of an Association of Free Churches cannot be a promise merely to "affirm"—in our heads—certain principles. A covenant is a promise to be there, with and for one another, as live bodies in a reflecting, counseling, advising body, making decisions—not on "issue statements" as though we were creedal churches but—about programs we want to develop for our free churches' decision to use or not use. We'd save a lot of money and time and hassle and have better church programs, if we also made it a rule of our bylaws: We won't undertake any common program unless at least half our congregations agree to do so, and we'll toss programs unless at least half our congregations elect to use them, within four or five years.

(5) If we made this change, our UUA elections would be—at once—much simpler and less expensive. Any members could urge their own elected officers, at home, to support candidates for UUA office. But the authority to vote would be in the hands of people vested with authentic authority by our congregations.

(6) We could greatly increase all our congregational officers' participation in our common concerns as an Association if we put much more emphasis on Annual District Meetings of officers, and agreed to meet in General Assemblies only every four years, for election of UUA officers.

(7) We ought, in our UUA and District bylaws, to prohibit any and all affiliate organizations from meeting, on the days of congregational officers' meetings, in any of the buildings used for these meetings, thus ending the affiliates' dominance.

Why care about a covenanted and healthy UUA?

Our congregations very much need to associate, formally and informally, with the capital "A" of the UUA and with the lower case "a" of neighborly gatherings, like SWUUSI, and also in *new* kinds of regular neighborly gatherings of our officers. Our elected lay and ordained offi-

115

cers need to meet and talk together, not *for* our members, but *of* what our congregations are trying to do and how we might do these things better.

Why? Because in the long run, we can only fulfill missions our congregations take up when our elected leaders meet regularly—formally to cooperate in developing the program resources we need, and also informally to learn, from one another, how to carry out our missions well, for the world's sake. Only we can teach each other how to gather and build strong, liberal free churches. Nobody else has a clue!

A new pattern: many smaller covenanted associations

We need newly to think smaller, less formally and more neighborly, of areas much smaller than our whole Association or Districts.

What if no UU congregations were isolated, even those that others would have to take a little commuter plane to visit? (I flew to serve two churches, a year each. Nothing to it.) Think of our extension congregations, many with a decades-long history of not-good patterns. To become thriving, the lay members of these congregations need to learn a good deal.

In our current Extension Program a new minister is dropped into the middle of a complex story that hasn't been going well, largely because the relational piece is missing from most small congregation's understanding of who they are. Members haven't seen that our worship services need to be super services for visitors looking for a good church, not just us "old hands," that our RE programs need to be super for new members' children who aren't here yet, not just our few children now, and so on.

But the fact that we have so many little isolated churches means, a relational piece is also missing from the self-understanding of other UU churches only a couple of hours, or less, away. Otherwise, ministers and lay officers of these churches would be there sometimes—listening and offering counsel, teaching members of the small church, just by their presence and conversation, what it means to be neighbors in a community of independent congregations.

Now, as in the past, even our ministers rarely think of the need of nearby congregations' lay officers for companionship with other officers.

Ministerial colleagues help each other, sure. But as UUs we don't call on our lay officers to take counsel with nearby churches, as our ancestors did. And I'm not talking about service on some darned District Committee, or even a cluster "board!" We'd be better off without all these committees or boards. I'm talking about elected church officers in a covenant of church friendship with other elected church officers, next door. And I don't mean only neighbors whose emphases or styles are exactly the same. An informal association of neighbors has to include all UU congregations in one another's reach, or it's not a covenant embracing healthy diversity but an exclusive cabal.

Suppose we began every new effort of our Extension or New Congregation Program this way: We gather the lay and ordained officers from three fairly nearby churches—with officers of the small congregation—and talk about the importance of getting healthy, super patterns set in a free church and how we do that, with the counsel of UU neighbors, but without "usurpation" of independence. The officers of all four congregations could work out a modest agreement to do neighboring: meet once in a while to do what associating free churches do—give and take counsel together. Lay officers of any church would learn so much from— say—just two four-hour meetings a year with all the lay and ordained officers of three other churches, where they live—not off at some distant and expensive "workshop."

Currently, we say an extension congregation enters a special relationship with "the UUA." What does that mean? Usually a "special relationship" with one UUA staffperson, or at best two or three, off and on, for three years. What are members of a weak church to learn from that, about relating to our community of congregations? In my experience, very little.

Certainly, if a small congregation gets UUA money to support their minister for three years, there should be some accountability for concrete steps toward strength and growth. But accountability should not be grossly complicated—lots of records, numbers and multiple graphs.

Questions of accountability for funds could well go something like this: Have you counseled with the finance committee of a nearby UU Church? An RE Committee? A Committee on Ministry? Has your whole congregation attended another UU church's Sunday service? And stayed

117

to find out how this church serves visitors? Have you borrowed another church's adult education materials? How many participated? Have you paired with another congregation to work for justice and mercy? How many participated? Let accountability be for breaking out of isolation and learning to be a healthy free church by neighboring, through experience with other super UUs.

Am I a crazy dreamer? Or might we learn again to be superbly covenanted, neighboring UU congregations? As independent as ever *and* members of a truly covenanted community of congregations? I think we would be super-glad if we did. For the results would be super.

But why limit this sort of neighboring to funded programs? How different our movement would be if we just dropped countless meetings of panels, commissions, special projects, committees, subcommittees, *ad infinitum*. What if all our ministers and lay officers met in groups of three, four or six area congregations for a day—or half a day—just twice a year? Two-hour drives to and from such a meeting are nothing to us, if they're not frequent and are significant, our agendas having to do with what concerns us. Helpful, interesting meetings would require a little thoughtful homework beforehand, but not much!

Suppose each congregation's officers covenant always to decide themselves, a week or so before each area meeting, which several individuals will give just three-minute responses to the following questions about their church:

Tell us about two programs of this current year in each of these areas of our church life: (1) worship, for any or all ages; (2) how our members choose, train and support our leaders; (3) education—especially of children and new members; and (4) and what members do in our church to work toward justice and mercy. Tell us about one program in each area you are proud of and feel good about, and mention the factors that make it good. Tell about one program in each area which is not going so well as you hoped, and mention the factors making it not so good.

So, that's the preparation part, eight oral reports of just three minutes each. Officers think some together about what they want to say and how to say it concisely, not in endless detail. At the meeting, listeners are asked to note, as they listen, any questions they want to ask about these programs or any insights or suggestions they have to offer because they have tried something similar.

After hearing these brief reports, the question becomes: Which of these matters do we need to talk about some more? In a meeting like this the asking for and the giving of rich counsel just flows. For when we get our churches' elected leaders talking freely, in a super format, about what works well and doesn't, they have to be pried apart. Or they will talk forever.

In the last half hour, then, lay and ministerial officers together could ask if a few meetings are needed during the next six months, not among these same officers, but among other lay leaders—say—of two Finance Committees, or three RE Committees, or two or three Committees on Ministry, any of whom can also give each other super counsel, because now their officers know the sort of help each congregation could really use. Such neighborly meetings as this would be altogether different from meetings some Planning Committee or workshop leader prepares, which seldom strike our churches "where they are."

In super meetings of a covenanted neighborly association, there have to be both "orderly rules" and spontaneity, high expectations of how we proceed *and* plenty of flexibility for the free spirit of mutual love to blow among us, as it will. There's a *there* there in this covenant. Live bodies meet, on time every time, ready to learn from and teach one another— with no supervision. And we'll be able to tell when our congregations are in such a covenant. For there will be then a super growth in the spirit of affection and forbearance in and among our independent congregations. And then—just down the road a way—growth in the numbers of people in our liberal free churches. For where the spirit of mutual love is strong and we work in good patterns, you can't keep new members out.

Reading List

Materials read (or re-read) in preparation for these lectures:

Acheson, R. J., *Radical Puritans in England 1550–1660* (Longman), 1990

Adams, James Luther, *On Being Human Religiously: Selected Essays in Religion and Society* (Beacon Press), 1976

Ahlstrom, Sydney E. and Carey, Jonathan, *An American Reformation: A Documentary History of Unitarian History* (Wesleyan University Press), 1985

Bancroft, Aaron, *Sermons on those Doctrines of the Gospel, and on those Constituent principles of the church which Christian Professors Have Made the Subject of Controversy* (William Manning & Son), 1822

Beach, Seth C., *A Brief History of the Last Three Pastorates of the First Parish in Dedham 1860–1888* (Published by the Parish), 1888

Boorstin, Daniel, *The Americans: The Colonial Experience* (Vintage Books), 1958

Bradford, William, *Of Plymouth Plantation 1620–1647* (Modern Library), 1981

Bush, Sargent, Jr., *The Writings of Thomas Hooker: Spiritual Adventure in Two Worlds* (University of Wisconsin Press), 1980

Capper, Charles and Wright, Conrad E., Eds., *Transient and Permanent: The Transcendentalist Movement and Its Contexts* (Massachusetts Historical Society), 1999

Clark, John Ruskin, *The Great Living System: Religion Emerging from the Sciences* (The Boxwood Press), 1977

Clarke, James Freeman, *The Christian Doctrine of Forgiveness of Sin: An Essay* (American Unitarian Association), 1874

—————, *Essentials and Non-Essentials in Religion, Six Lectures Delivered in the Music Hall, Boston* (American Unitarian Association), 1878

—————, *Events and Epochs in Religious History* (James R. Osgood and Company), 1881

—————, *Self-Culture: Physical, Intellectual, Moral and Spiritual* (Houghton, Mifflin and Company), 1889

Cooke, George Willis, *Unitarianism in America: A History of Its Origin and Development* (American Unitarian Association), 1910

Cousins, Norman, *'In God We Trust': The Religious Beliefs and Ideas of the American Founding Fathers* (Harper & Brothers Publishers), 1958

—————, *Dedham Pulpit or, Sermons by the Pastors of the First Church in Dedham in the XVIIth and XVIIIth Centuries* (Perkins & Marvin), 1840

Dunning, Albert E., *Congregationalists in America: A Popular History of Their Origin* (The Pilgrim Press), 1894

Elazar, Daniel J., *Covenant & Polity in Biblical Israel: Volume I of the Covenant Tradition in Politics* (Transaction Publishers), 1995

—————, *Covenant & Commonwealth: From Christian Separation through the Protestant Reformation: Volume II of the Covenant Tradition in Politics* (Transaction Publishers), 1996

—————, *Covenant & Constitutionalism: The Great Frontier and the Matrix of Federal Democracy: Volume III of The Covenant Tradition in Politics* (Transaction Publishers), 1998

—————, *Covenant and Civil Society: The Constitutional Matrix of Modern Democracy: Volume IV of The Covenant Tradition in Politics* (Transaction Publishers), 1998

Fenn, Dan Huntington, Ed., *Theism: The Implication of Experience by William Wallace Fenn* (William L. Bauhan, Inc.), 1969

Firth, C. H., *Oliver Cromwell and the Rule of the Puritans in England* (Putnam), 1947 edition

Frothingham, Octavius Brooks, *Memoir of William Henry Channing* (Houghton, Mifflin and Company), 1886

Gatta, John, *Gracious Laughter, The Meditative Wit of Edward Taylor* (University of Missouri Press), 1989

George, Timothy, *John Robinson and the English Separatist Tradition* (Mercer

University Press), 1982

Hambrick-Stowe, Charles E., *The Practice of Piety: Puritan Devotional Disciplines in Seventeenth-Century New England* (University of North Carolina Press), 1982

——————, Ed., *Anne Bradstreet and Edward Taylor: Early Meditative Poetry* (Paulist Press), 1988

Hartshorne, Charles, *A Natural Theology for Our Time* (Open Court), 1967

Hedge, Frederic Henry, *Ways of the Spirit, And Other Essays* (Roberts Brothers), 1878

Hill, Christopher, *Puritanism & Revolution: The English Revolution of the 17th Century* (Schocken Books), paperback edition 1964

Hosmer, J. K., Ed., *Winthrop's Journal "History of New England,"* *1630–1649* (Charles Scribner's Sons), 1908

Howe, Daniel Walker, *The Unitarian Conscience: Harvard Moral Philosophy, 1805–1861* (Harvard University Press), 1970

Kring, Walter Donald, *Henry Whitney Bellows* (Skinner House), 1979

Lamson, Alvan, *Sermons by Alvan Lamson* (Crosby, Nichols, and Company), 1857

Livermore, Abiel Abbot, *Discourses by Abiel Abbot Livermore* (D.C. Colesworthy), 1857

Lockridge, Kenneth A., *A New England Town: The First Hundred Years Dedham, Massachusetts, 1638–1736* (W. W. Norton & Company, Inc.), 1970

Lowance, Mason L., *The Language of Canaan: Metaphor and Symbol in New England from the Puritans to the Transcendentalists* (Harvard University Press), 1980

McGiffert, Arthur Cushman, Jr., *Pilot of a Liberal Faith: Samuel Atkins Eliot 1862–1950* (Skinner House Books), 1976

McGiffert, Michael, *God's Plot: The Paradoxes of Puritan Piety* (University of Massachusetts Press), 1972

Martineau, James, *Sermons* (E. T. Whitfield), 1857

Mayhew, Jonathan, *Seven Sermons*, first printed 1748 (Arno Press), 1969

Mead, Sidney E., *The Nation with the Soul of a Church* (Harper & Row, Publishers), 1975

Morgan, Irvonwy, *Prince Charles's Puritan Chaplain* (George Allen &

Unwin Ltd), 1957

Morison, Samuel Eliot, *The Founding of Harvard College* (Harvard University Press), 1935

Olds, Mason, *American Religious Humanism* (Fellowship of Religious Humanists), 1996

Perry, Ralph Barton, *Puritanism and Democracy* (The Vanguard Press), 1944

Petit, Norman, *The Heart Prepared: Grace and Conversion in Puritan Spiritual Life* (Yale University Press), 1966

Pope, Robert G., *The Half-Way Covenant: Church Membership in Puritan New England* (Princeton University Press), 1969

Preston, John, *The Golden Sceptre Held Forth to The Humble, Preached at Cambridge, A.D. 1625* (SoliDeo Gloria Reprint), 1990

——————, *The Breast Plate of Faith and Love* (The Banner of Truth Trust, facsimile of 1630 publication), 1979

Royce, Josiah, *The Problem of Christianity with a new introduction by John E. Smith* (University of Chicago Press), 1968

Schenk, W., *The Concern for Social Justice in the Puritan Revolution* (Longmans, Green and Co. Ltd.), 1948

Schweninger, Lee, *John Winthrop* (Twayne Publishers), 1990

Seaver, Paul S., *Wallington's World: A Puritan Artisan in Seventeenth-Century London* (Stanford University Press), 1985

Stout, Harry S., *The New England Soul: Preaching and Religious Culture in Colonial New England* (Oxford University Press), 1986

Thoreau, Henry David, *A Week on the Concord and Merrimack Rivers; Walden; or, Life in the Woods* (Library of America)

——————, *The Maine Woods* (Library of America)

——————, *Cape Cod* (Library of America)

Walker, Williston, Richard A. Norris, David W. Lotz, and Robert T. Handy, *A History of the Christian Church: Fourth Edition* (Charles Scribner's Sons), 1985

Williams, Selma R., *Kings, Commoners & Colonists: Puritan Politics in Old and New England 1603–1660* (Atheneum), 1974

Wright, Conrad, *The Beginnings of Unitarianism in America* (Beacon Press), 1955

—————, *The Liberal Christians: Essays on American Unitarian History* (Unitarian Universalist Association), 1970

—————, *Religion in American Life: Selected Readings* (Houghton Mifflin Company), 1972

—————, Ed., *A Stream of Light: A Sesquicentennial History of American Unitarianism* (Unitarian Universalist Association), 1975

—————, *Congregational Polity: A Historical Survey of Unitarian Universalist Practice* (Skinner House Books), 1997

—————, Ed., *American Unitarianism 1805–1865* (Massachusetts Historical Society and Northeastern University Press), 1989

—————, Ed., *Massachusetts and the New Nation* (Massachusetts Historical Society), 1992

————— and Capper, Charles, Eds., *The Transformation of Charity in Postrevolutionary New England* (Northeastern University Press), 1992

CPSIA information can be obtained at www.ICGtesting.com
Printed in the USA
LVOW040145130812

293943LV00003B/25/A